# I AM A FEMINIST

## Claiming the F-Word in Turbulent Times

MONIQUE POLAK

illustrations by
Meags Fitzgerald

ORCA BOOK PUBLISHERS

**Library and Archives Canada Cataloguing in Publication**

Polak, Monique, author
I am a feminist: claiming the f-word in turbulent times / Monique Polak.

(Orca issues)
Includes bibliographical references and index.
Issued in print and electronic formats.
ISBN 978-1-4598-1892-7 (softcover).—ISBN 978-1-4598-1893-4 (PDF).—
ISBN 978-1-4598-1894-1 (EPUB)

1. Feminism—Juvenile literature. I. Title.
HQ1155.P64 2018          j305.42          C2018-904767-4
                         C2018-904768-2

Issued in print and electronic formats.
ISBN 978-1-4598-1892-7 (softcover).—ISBN 978-1-4598-1893-4 (PDF).—
ISBN 978-1-4598-1894-1 (EPUB)

Library of Congress Control Number: 2018954084
Simultaneously published in Canada and the United States in 2019

**Summary:** This nonfiction book encourages teens to stand up for equality and speak out against injustice.

Orca Book Publishers gratefully acknowledges the support for its publishing programs provided by the following agencies: the Government of Canada, the Canada Council for the Arts and the Province of British Columbia through the BC Arts Council and the Book Publishing Tax Credit.

**Interior illustrations by Meags Fitzgerald**

Edited by Sarah N. Harvey
Design by Teresa Bubela
Cover photo by Rebecca Wellman
Cover illustrations by Meags Fitzgerald

ORCA BOOK PUBLISHERS
orcabook.com

Printed and bound in China.

22  21  20  19  •  4  3  2  1

*For Viva Singer, Debra Arbec and Michele Luchs—hoop sisters.*
*With love and gratitude.*

# CONTENTS

FEMINISM IS THE RADICAL NOTION THAT WOMEN ARE PEOPLE.

—Marie Shear,
Writer & Editor

*Introduction*

# WHAT IS FEMINISM, AND WHY DO YOU NEED TO READ THIS BOOK?

**"D**o you consider yourself a feminist?"

I put that question to thirteen-year-old Samantha. We were having tea with Samantha's grandma, who lives down the street from me in Montreal, Quebec. Samantha, who was going into ninth grade in Vancouver, British Columbia, was at the tail end of a two-week visit to Montreal.

"I'm not sure," Samantha said. "But I do believe women should have equal rights."

"In that case," I pointed out, "you are a feminist."

According to the *Oxford English Dictionary (OED)*, *feminism* is "the advocacy of women's rights on the ground of the equality of the sexes." Who can argue with that?

And yet when Canadian prime minister Justin Trudeau declared, "I am a feminist" during his address to the United Nations women's conference in March 2016, it made front-page news around the world. "I am going to keep saying loud and clearly that I am a feminist. Until it is met with a shrug," Trudeau explained.

In 2016 Canadian prime minister Justin Trudeau made international news when he declared, "I am a feminist."

Not all young—or, for that matter, older—women and men are as comfortable as Trudeau is when it comes to identifying themselves as feminists. Some think that even saying the word *feminism* out loud makes them man haters!

In their book *ManifestA: Young Women, Feminism, and the Future*, Jennifer Baumgardner and Amy Richards suggest that some people feel threatened by the word *feminism* because it is "a word of great power."

The term *f-word* is sometimes used to refer to feminism, a "humorous" way of saying that using the word *feminism*, or declaring oneself a feminist, is somehow rude or wrong.

But thank goodness that's changing! Here's proof: in 2017, the *Merriam-Webster Dictionary* declared *feminism* its word of the year—because it was the most looked-up word on its online dictionary.

As part of my research for this book, I spoke to girls, women, boys and men about feminism. Because I live in Montreal, most of the people I interviewed live here too—but I believe that their experiences reflect those of many people worldwide. Every single adult woman I spoke with reported having experienced some form of *sexism* in her life.

Evelyn Sacks, a retired schoolteacher who died in 2018, just two months short of her 100th birthday, remembered being paid considerably less than her male colleagues, despite the fact that they worked the same number of hours and taught the same number of students.

Elisabeth Telford-Klerks recalled that when she was studying nursing in Toronto, Ontario, in 1959, she and the other nurses in training (all female) had to stand aside and let the doctors (all male) onto the elevator first.

Today, at the college where I teach in Montreal, male and female teachers are paid equal salaries. And most of us know as many female doctors as male ones. Though feminists have made huge, important strides (you'll learn more about their work in chapter 1), inequality between the sexes persists. **Misogyny**, which means prejudice against girls or women, remains far too common.

Consider the following examples of inequality between the sexes: On average, most women still do not earn equal pay for equal work. In Canada in 2015, women earned eighty-seven cents for every dollar a man earned. In the same year, American women fared even worse, earning only eighty cents for every dollar earned by American men. Women are four times more likely than men to be victims of *intimate partner violence* (sometimes called domestic violence). And in at least ten countries,

During a visit to Montreal, QC, 13-year-old Samantha learned that her grandmother, Joanne Morgan, co-founded the women's studies program at Vanier College.

including Cambodia, Ethiopia, Haiti and Nepal, it is difficult and often impossible for girls to attend school.

When I asked Samantha if she had ever experienced sexism, it didn't take her long to come up with an answer. "The girls in my class are more athletic than the boys. I had this teacher who selected the boys to do the heavy lifting. It kind of bothered me— even if I didn't really want to help lift furniture!" she told me.

In 2016, Samantha, a competitive swimmer since the age of eight, came in fourth in her age group in British Columbia in butterfly. "You have to be strong and confident to do the butterfly," she explained. Because it requires tremendous muscular strength, the butterfly stroke tends to be associated with male rather than female swimmers. "I've noticed lately," Samantha said, "that fewer girls my age are doing the butterfly. They seem to be less motivated." Some girls give up the butterfly because they worry it will give them "man shoulders." Of course, for boys, "man shoulders" are a good thing. Some coaches, too, may contribute to the problem by failing to encourage girls to continue doing a stroke that is considered masculine. All this serves as another indication that sexism exists—even in the lap lane.

"Did you know," I asked Samantha, "that your grandma was one of the founders of the women's studies program at Vanier College here in Montreal?"

Samantha's head spun around to look at her grandma, as if she was seeing her for the first time.

Then Samantha's grandma told us how she became a feminist: "I married at the age of twenty-two, and I was home with four small children when I read Betty Friedan's book *The Feminine Mystique*. It blew me away. I tried to tell my best friend about the book, but she didn't want to hear about it."

Friedan's book is often credited with ushering in what is known as the second wave of feminism (you'll learn more about that in chapter 1 too). In her book, Friedan used the phrase "the problem that has no name" to refer to the plight of women in society. Friedan argued there was more to a woman's life than looking after her husband and kids.

*Betty Friedan's 1963 book* The Feminine Mystique *is often credited for ushering in the second wave of feminism.*

More recently, feminists such as bell hooks have criticized Friedan for focusing only on white women. hooks was one of the first feminist scholars to study *intersectionality* (the overlap between sexism, racism and classism—more about that in chapter 6).

Intersectionality looks at the overlap of identities such as race, gender, class and sexuality. All women, including the most marginalized, must be included in the struggle for equality.

She observed that many black women in Friedan's time were in the workforce, most of them employed in low-prestige jobs that paid poorly. Friedan's views did not help these women or other women of color. Not only were they already working, but many were trapped in jobs white women did not want.

If you are living in relative comfort in North America—meaning you have food, clothing, a safe place to live and access to health care and education—you may also grow up thinking there's no need for feminism.

But there is.

Feminism is not a done deal.

In North America, women have the right to vote, and most women have access to legal abortion. Girls can go on to study and work in the fields of their choice. But there is still plenty of inequality between the sexes.

When I started to do the research for this book, I quickly realized there was a lot I did not know about issues related to feminism. Keep reading—and I promise you will learn a lot too.

But maybe you're wondering why you should read *my* book about feminism. After all, I'm a middle-aged white woman. What could you and I possibly have in common?

Let me share a little more of my own story. I was born in 1960. Though my parents met at law school in the Netherlands, my mom never practised as a lawyer. Instead, she stayed home to raise her three children. I still remember how, on Friday nights, my dad would call my mom upstairs to give her what he called her "allowance"—enough cash to pay for groceries and other expenses for the week ahead.

As a girl growing up, I loved writing, and I often played "school" in our basement, but I never really imagined that I would have a career. Instead, I thought I would fall madly in love and live happily ever after. I have been married—and divorced—twice.

As a young woman I experienced intimate partner violence. To a large extent I blamed myself for tolerating (and perhaps even inciting) the violence for several years before I was able to leave the relationship.

In my work as a journalist, I have developed a specialty in writing about intimate partner violence. When I tell the women I interview that I was once where they are, it often becomes easier for them to open up and share their stories with me.

In the late 1960s, feminists began to use the phrase "The personal is political." I had heard that phrase many times. But it was not until I was writing this book that I realized how much that statement applied to my experience too.

Despite my personal struggles, I recognize my own privilege as a white, heterosexual, educated, financially secure, **cisgender** woman. (*Cisgender* means that a person's sense of identity and gender corresponds with their birth sex.) In this book we'll return to the question of privilege, and to the importance of taking an intersectional approach to feminism, which aims to improve the lives of all women.

Many of my friends who attended college and university took women's-studies courses. I never did. Life made me a feminist.

Working on this book has also made me understand the urgent need for activism. It isn't enough to talk about feminism. We need to take action by standing up not only for ourselves, but also, and especially, for women who are part of **marginalized** communities, meaning they are socially disadvantaged and often discriminated against.

This book is for Samantha and all the young people like her who are not sure if they are feminists and who, like me, have many questions but who hope for a better world for all of us, regardless of our gender, sexual preference, race, religion, class or where we happen to live.

I am a feminist.

What about you?

In March 2017 participants in the International Women's Day March in Los Angeles, CA, demanded equal rights for women and objected to the Trump administration's stand on women's rights.

# WAVES OF FEMINISM

## FIRST WAVE: 1830s to early 1900s

Votes for women—all over the world, suffragists stand up for a woman's right to vote

Property rights—women demand the right to own property

1918— Marie Stopes advocates gender equality in marriage. Her book *Married Love* is banned in the US until 1931

## SECOND WAVE: 1960s to late 1980s

Women rally for equal pay for equal work

SAME WORK SAME PAY! $=$

Reproductive rights become an important issue in the fight for equality. In 1960 the birth control pill is approved in the U.S.

1963— Book by Betty Friedan leads to the formation of many feminist organizations

THE FEMININE MYSTIQUE BETTY FRIEDAN

## THIRD WAVE: 1990s to 2000s

The Riot Grrrl movement creates zines and art that talk about rape, patriarchy, sexuality and female empowerment

Intersectionality becomes a defining issue for feminists

2000— *Feminism is for Everybody* by bell hooks introduces feminist politics in an accessible format. "There can be no love without justice."

## FOURTH WAVE: now

Hashtag feminism focuses on exposing and ending street and workplace harassment, body-shaming, campus sexual assault and rape culture

Feminists support body-, trans- and sex-positivity

2017—The Women's March on Washington inspires women's marches around the world

*Chapter One*

# RIDE THE WAVE: THE HISTORY OF FEMINISM

I chose *Ride the Wave* as the title for this chapter because I liked the sound of it, but when I looked up what it really means I decided I was on the right track. "Riding the wave" means to enjoy a period of success and good fortune.

The feminist movement is often described as happening in waves. Every one of us benefits from the progress made by the women (and their **allies**) who came before us in the fight for equality between the sexes. In this way, we are still riding the wave.

Most people describe three waves, but recently there has been talk of a fourth—and sometimes even a fifth—wave.

It's human nature to take the good things in our lives for granted. For example, when I go to the polling station at the school near my house, I do not give much thought to the days when women were not allowed to cast votes. I don't think about the women who fought for **suffrage** (the right to vote in political elections).

That's why I'm about to remind you of all that has been achieved—so far—by the feminists who came before us.

Pictured here at Ottawa's Rideau Hall, members of Canada's National Council of Women supported women's right to vote.

## FIRST-WAVE FEMINISM

*First-wave feminism* took place between the 1830s and early 1900s. Women realized they would need political power to bring about societal change. That's why early feminists fought for suffrage, and it explains why these women were known as *suffragists* and later *suffragettes*.

Around the world the suffrage movement was connected to the *temperance* campaign, a movement advocating moderation in the consumption of alcohol or total abstinence from it. People— men as well as women—recognized that alcohol contributed to societal problems. If a woman's husband got drunk and spent the family's grocery money on liquor, or if he beat her, there was little she could do about it. At the time, women were seldom granted divorces, and few could support themselves and their children financially. In those days women could not even own property.

Canada's first suffrage association was formed in Toronto, Ontario, in 1877. In order to avoid causing a stir, the group called itself a women's literary society! By 1914 the Canadian suffrage movement had 10,000 members—some of them men. Ten thousand may seem like a big number, but it was only two-tenths of a percent of the country's adult population at the time. For the most part, the suffrage movement was a peaceful campaign. Suffragists petitioned government officials and organized lectures. In 1914, activist Nellie McClung rented Winnipeg's Walker Theatre, where she and her fellow suffragists enacted a mock parliament run by women. This was a creative way to show society that women wanted an equal voice in government.

Nellie McClung was an important Canadian suffragist. She came up with a creative way to demonstrate that women deserve an equal voice in government.

World War I (1914–1918) also helped the suffrage movement. With so many men fighting overseas, women not only took charge of their families, but many also took over men's jobs, another indication of how capable women were—and how deserving of the right to vote.

By 1918 most Canadian women over the age of twenty-one had the right to vote in federal elections. These included women of color but, sadly, not Indigenous men and women, who were excluded from voting in federal elections until 1960. Also by 1918, most Canadian women had provincial *franchise*

American suffragists ride in a hay wagon during a 1913 suffrage parade.

(franchise is another term that refers to the right to vote) as well. Quebec was the last Canadian province to give women the right to vote.

Quebec politician and journalist Henri Bourassa was a vocal opponent of women's suffrage. He warned that allowing women to vote would turn them into "veritable women-men."

In the United States, Sojourner Truth, whose birth name was Isabella Baumfree, was an early advocate of rights for women and blacks. In 1826, at the age of twenty-nine, she escaped a life of slavery. Sojourner Truth is best known for her impassioned "Ain't I A Woman?" speech, which she delivered in 1851 at the Ohio Women's Rights Convention. Most American women were granted the right to vote in 1920 with the ratification of the Nineteenth Amendment to the U.S. Constitution. As in Canada, American suffragists had been lobbying for many years. Women's suffrage was an important part of the discussion at the Seneca Falls Convention, held in 1848 in Seneca Falls, New York. This convention is considered the first women's rights conference.

Like Indigenous men and women in Canada, Native Americans also had to wait to get the right to vote. That finally happened in 1924 when the United States passed the Indian Citizenship Act. Even then, some states, such as Arizona and New Mexico, resisted and did not allow their Indigenous population to vote until 1948.

*Born into slavery, Sojourner Truth fought for the rights of women and black people.*

## DETERMINED TO BECOME A DOCTOR— AND GET THE VOTE FOR CANADIAN WOMEN

### Emily Stowe was a feminist!

Emily Stowe is considered the founder of Canada's suffrage movement. Emily's mother was a Quaker, a Christian religious group that believes in the equality of women and men. At the age of 20, Emily became Canada's first woman school principal. After her husband fell ill with tuberculosis, and Emily had to do more to help support her family, she decided to become a doctor. Her application to study medicine at the University of Toronto was rejected. So she enrolled at the New York Medical College for Women. Emily's daughter, Augusta Stowe Gullen, became a doctor too. Augusta graduated from Victoria University, Toronto, in 1883, the first woman to receive medical training in Canada.

VOTES FOR WOMEN

Rosa Parks is fingerprinted after being arrested for boycotting public transportation in Montgomery, AL, February 1956.

## SECOND-WAVE FEMINISM

*Second-wave feminism* began in the early 1960s and lasted until the late 1980s. The movement started in the United States but quickly traveled throughout the **developed world** (countries where there is a high level of industrial activity and where citizens can earn good wages). It was sparked, in part, by the Civil Rights Movement (1954–1968), which fought to end racial segregation and discrimination against African Americans. Although women played an important role in the Civil Rights Movement, many of them felt they had been overshadowed by men. These women complained of gender discrimination as well as **sexual harassment**. So black women started their own feminist groups, in which they focused on issues including access to health care and reproductive rights. Unfortunately, these women were criticized by some members of the Black Liberation movement, who called them "race traitors." Early black feminists were also discriminated against by white feminists. During these years, black women were seldom invited to sit on panels at events promoting feminism.

Betty Friedan's 1963 book *The Feminine Mystique* also played a major role in ushering in the second wave of feminism. The book quickly became a bestseller. Inspired by Friedan's views and findings that many women were dissatisfied with their role as full-time homemakers, second-wave feminists focused initially on workplace inequality.

*Students in a home economics class in 1959 learn skills meant to prepare them to be wives and mothers.*

In 1960 only 38 percent of American women worked outside the home. Most were limited to jobs perceived as traditionally female: teaching, nursing or doing secretarial work. Others worked as domestics, cleaning other people's homes and offices. In the United States in 1960 only 6 percent of doctors were women, 3 percent of lawyers were women, and less than 1 percent of engineers were women. Things have changed a lot since those days. By 2017, in the United States, 40 percent of doctors were women, 37.4 percent of lawyers were women and 16.2 percent of those employed in the architectural and engineering sectors were women. Unfortunately, women still lag behind in what are known as the *STEM* (science, technology, engineering and math) professions.

*Consciousness-raising groups* became popular during feminism's second wave. Women met, often in each other's homes, to discuss issues such as work, family life, education and sex. For many of them, these meetings marked the first time they had spoken openly about such subjects with other women.

*Buttons like this one have been used since 1969 by the Redstockings, a feminist group founded in New York City.*

Women also began campaigning for the legalization of abortion. They organized speak-outs, in which women spoke publicly about rape (an experience many had been reluctant to share) and the experience of having had illegal abortions. Although abortion became legal in many countries because women fought for this right, legal, safe abortions and reproductive rights are currently under attack worldwide.

In 1960 the United States Food and Drug Administration approved the birth control pill for contraceptive use, freeing

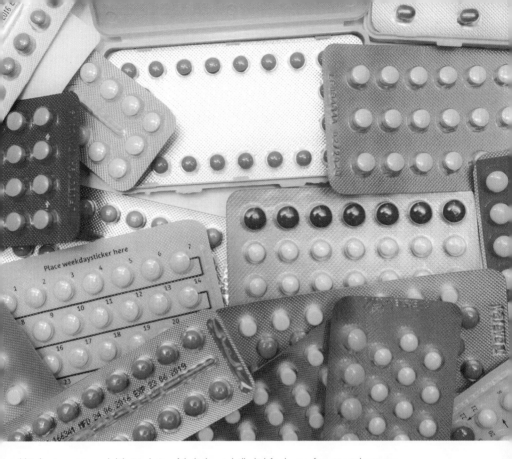

A lot of controversy surrounded the introduction of the birth control pill, which freed women from unwanted pregnancy.

many women from unwanted pregnancies. By 1965, 6.5 million American women were using the birth control pill.

There was no shortage of controversy surrounding the introduction of the birth control pill. In 1968 Pope Paul VI declared his opposition to the pill. And in 1988 the original high-dose birth control pill was taken off the market and replaced by newer pills with a lower risk of ovarian cancer.

Today, many women who spent years on the birth control pill—including me—wonder why we were never warned about the associated medical risks, which include a higher incidence of breast and cervical cancer, heart attacks and strokes.

Why, we also wonder, has birth control always been considered largely a woman's responsibility?

A *vasectomy* is a simple surgical procedure performed on a man that prevents the release of sperm during ejaculation. Vasectomies are usually reversible. Why don't more men get vasectomies and, by so doing, reduce their partners' reliance on synthetic hormones, IUDs or getting their "tubes tied"? Hopefully, as more men become feminists, we will see change in this area too.

## MS. MAGAZINE: STILL NOT RUNNING OUT OF THINGS TO SAY

Until *Ms. Magazine* hit the newsstands in 1972, the pages of women's magazines were filled with recipes, makeup tips and advice for dealing with romantic and family issues. Feminist journalist Gloria Steinem was the co-founder of *Ms. Magazine.* It first appeared in 1971 as a one-shot insert in *New York Magazine.* The first regular issue came out in July 1972 and featured Wonder Woman on its cover. American news anchor Harry Reasoner predicted, "I'll give it six months before they run out of things to say." Reasoner was wrong. *Ms. Magazine* continues to be published quarterly. It has 110,000 subscribers and accepts only "mission-driven advertisements from primarily non-profit, non-partisan organizations." In other words, it's not taking money from companies that just want to make readers buy their products.

American writer and activist Rebecca Walker came up with the term third-wave feminism.

## THIRD-WAVE FEMINISM

*Third-wave feminism* began in the 1990s, when many people started saying we were living in a postfeminist society. American writer, activist and feminist Rebecca Walker coined the term "third-wave feminism" in a 1992 article for *Ms. Magazine*, in which she proclaimed, "I am the Third Wave."

The words *intersectional* and **multiperspectival** (did you even know that was a word?) are sometimes used to describe feminism's third wave. Third-wave feminists like Walker rebelled against certain elements of second-wave feminism. In particular, they felt that the earlier waves of feminism focused too much on the needs of white, educated, middle-class women—and not enough on women who were marginalized by race, poverty, disability, age and sexual expression.

Third-wave feminists believe that all women must have a place—and a voice—in the feminist movement. To use the words of bell hooks, one of the leaders of third-wave feminism, "Feminism is for everybody."

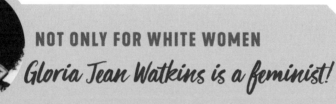

## NOT ONLY FOR WHITE WOMEN
### Gloria Jean Watkins is a feminist!

Gloria Jean Watkins was born in Hopkinsville, Kentucky, in 1952. You've probably never heard of her. That's because Watkins wrote under the pen name bell hooks. She chose the pseudonym based on the name of her maternal great-grandmother, Bell Blair Hooks. When she attended Stanford University in the 1970s, hooks was the only black woman in her feminist classrooms. That was also when she became aware that racist biases shaped feminist thinking. While attending Stanford, hooks wrote the first draft of the book that became *ain't i a woman: black women and feminism*, which was eventually published in 1981. You are probably wondering why hooks does not capitalize the initial letters of her first and last names. She has explained that it's because what is most important is "the substance of my books, not who is writing them."

Left: *This protest sign reminds us of the importance of intersectionality, and that we can only create change by working together.*

## GETTING WITH THE TIMES

In October 2017 the *New York Times* hired Jessica Bennett to be its first gender editor. Bennett is the author of *Feminist Fight Club: An Office Survival Manual for a Sexist Workplace* and had worked as a freelancer for the newspaper. Her job is to look at all news—whether it's about gender, sexuality, health or even science and politics—through an intersectional lens. As Bennett told *Teen Vogue:* "The reality is that institutions, and old-school media institutions, were primarily created by and for white men. But that has changed."

## FOURTH-WAVE FEMINISM

*Fourth-wave feminism* is happening right now! In 2009 Jessica Valenti, founder of *Feministing*, an online community for young feminists, suggested that the fourth wave of feminism was taking place online. Online communities and **hashtag activism** make it possible for young women around the world to create community and engage in meaningful discussion and debate.

The fourth wave of feminism is **sex positive, trans inclusive, body positive** and **size inclusive**. Fourth-wave feminists are opposed to **slut shaming** (criticizing a woman for her sexual desire). They are working to ensure the rights of transgender and gender non-conforming individuals, and they reject the notion that there is only one acceptable body type.

## TEENAGE FEMINIST IS THE BOMB

### Julie Zeilinger is a feminist!

Julie Zeilinger was 16 when she started her blog *The FBomb* in 2009. Today *The FBomb* reaches 30,000 readers! Zeilinger came up with the idea for the blog when she started looking at other feminist blogs such as *Jezebel* and *Feministing* and realized they were directed mostly at women who were in their twenties or older. "I wanted to find my own community. I saw a real need for it," Zeilinger told me in a phone interview from her home in New York City. In 2014 Zeilinger partnered with the Women's Media Center, which was founded in 2005 by Jane Fonda, Robin Morgan and Gloria Steinem. Zeilinger says Steinem has been an important mentor and role model for her: "She is incredibly supportive of intergenerational feminism. She's conscientious about including all voices. She takes what she does seriously, but she doesn't take herself too seriously. She's warm and funny—especially in hard times."

*Chapter Two*

# WE'RE ALL IN THIS TOGETHER: GIRLS AROUND THE WORLD

have an interview with Homa Hoodfar. We are meeting at a café near her home in Montreal.

Everyone I know in Montreal has heard of Homa Hoodfar. Most of us signed the petition, begun by one of her colleagues at Concordia University, demanding that she be released from Evin Prison, the most notorious jail in Tehran, Iran.

In September 2016, thanks in part to the outcry from the international community, Hoodfar, who teaches anthropology, was freed after 112 days in prison. You must be wondering what she was charged with. Was she a thief? A cyber-criminal? Maybe even a murderer?

No. Hoodfar was accused of "dabbling in feminism." At the time of her arrest she was in Tehran doing research for a book about women in Iranian politics during the early twentieth century.

"They took me from court to jail. I didn't have my medication for my blood condition. I couldn't sleep. The light was on all the time. The food was awful. I was mostly alone in my cell," Hoodfar told me.

In 2016, on a return visit to her native Iran, Concordia University professor Homa Hoodfar was imprisoned for "dabbling in feminism."

The prison guards tried to intimidate Hoodfar. "They told me, *You'll have to do ten years in prison and we'll send your dead body back to Canada.*" But although Hoodfar was exhausted, ill and hungry, she found the courage to stand up to those guards. "I told them, *Fine. I'm sixty-five. I've lived the life I've chosen.*"

Some of the things Hoodfar told me that May morning, eight months after her release from Evin Prison, made me cry.

Prison authorities knew how much writing meant to Hoodfar. That was why she was forbidden to have pen and paper. Hoodfar found another way to record her thoughts and feelings. "I used the tail of my toothbrush to write on the wall. The act of writing helped me memorize my ideas," she explained.

## RAISED BY A FEMINIST DAD

*Homa Hoodfar is a feminist!*

Homa Hoodfar credits her father, Abbas Hoodfar, for making her a feminist: "He told me, *Women can do anything men can do and probably more so. He thought women were more complete human beings because they gave life and have a caring capacity.*" Growing up in Iran, Hoodfar remembers that her grandmother (her father's mother) tried to prevent her from climbing trees. "She said, *Girls don't do that.* She ordered me to stop, but I wouldn't. When I complained to my father, he just laughed," Hoodfar recalls.

Why did I choose to start this chapter with Hoodfar's story? Because Homa Hoodfar was imprisoned for being a feminist. Because two of my closest friends—one a successful financial analyst and single mom in her forties; the other an art history teacher in her sixties—have told me they are not comfortable calling themselves feminists. One of them said, "Being a woman has never prevented me from getting anything I wanted in life."

Unfortunately, that is not the case for many girls and women.

For girls in many countries it is difficult and often impossible to attend school. In developing countries, girls—most of them under the age of fifteen—and women are dying from preventable causes related to pregnancy, unsafe abortions and childbirth. Girls in thirty countries have been subjected to genital mutilation, a painful surgery that has no known health benefits but which has serious short- and long-term complications. During war, girls and women are routinely raped and used as sex slaves. Indigenous women are at high risk of all types of violence—and too little

MONIQUE POLAK

is being done about it. (You'll learn more about the particular challenges faced by Indigenous women in chapter 6.)

Researching this chapter made me sad, angry and often sick to my stomach. But it also deepened my commitment to feminism— and to fighting for equality for every single person on Earth.

Be warned: Reading this chapter may have a similar effect on you. To be honest, I hope it does. Because then you may be inspired to take action to help ensure true equality for girls and women around the world.

# ACCESS TO EDUCATION

School—who needs it?

The answer is all of us. Having an education is like having a passport. An education makes it possible to go places. And I'm not talking about travel (though that is nice too). I am talking about opportunities.

Every semester, on the first day of class, I remind my students that being in school is a privilege, one that many young people (especially girls) around the world do not have. I describe the elementary school I visited in Diani Beach, Kenya, in 2011. The walls were cardboard, the textbooks were thirty years old, and most of the students were HIV positive. Yet even with all that, those students in Diani Beach felt lucky because they *were* in school.

In developing countries like Kenya, girls have less access to education than boys do. The reasons are complicated. In rural communities, the nearest school can be a four- or five-hour walk away. A lengthy walk can pose many dangers—especially for girls, who are at greater risk than boys of violence, rape and kidnapping.

Gender norms also play a huge role in reducing girls' access to education. When a family is poor, girls often have to stay home to

## MAKING GIRLS' EDUCATION A NUMBER-ONE PRIORITY

Thanks to a not-for-profit organization called She's the First, American students are helping girls in developing countries attend school and, in many cases, become the first in their families to graduate from high school and even college. She's the First was founded in 2009 by Tammy Tibbetts and Christen Brandt (pictured below). The organization's motto is "A girl with an education is unstoppable." Tibbetts and Brandt were the first in their own families to graduate from college. They launched She's the First with a YouTube video. The organization educates American students about the issue of girls' access to education and helps them organize fundraising events. To date, She's the First has raised over $2 million to support girls' access to education and has sent 500 girls to school in 10 countries, including Scholars at Shanti Bhavan in India (pictured above).

help with chores, such as fetching water and looking after younger siblings. Even when school is free there are related expenses, such as the cost of uniforms, school supplies and bus fare. Faced with deciding which of their children will go to school, most families in developing countries choose their sons over their daughters.

According to Plan International, a **not-for-profit organization** that supports social justice for children, 62 million girls around the world are not in school—and millions more are fighting for the opportunity to remain in school.

A working paper issued by the World Bank pointed out that "for every year a girl stays in school, her income can increase by ten to twenty percent."

## STRAIGHT TALK ABOUT PERIODS!

Even in North America, menstruation is a subject most people avoid talking about. Menstruation is an even more taboo topic in developing countries such as South Sudan. In that country's East Equatoria state, many girls and women cannot afford sanitary pads. Instead, they use leaves, paper or old clothing.

Sixteen-year-old Nyawut misses at least one day of school every month. "I miss classes because the rags I use become too worn. I worry that my clothes will get wet when I am sitting at my desk. I feel dirty," says Nyawut. Plan International, a not-for-profit global organization, distributes "dignity kits" to young women in South Sudan. The kits contain washable, reusable sanitary pads. Plan International also provides information sessions to educate young women about menstruation and reproductive health.

These girls are attending school at the Sam Ouandja refugee camp in the Central African Republic. Many of these girls had never attended school before coming to the refugee camp.

Today, the best-known advocate for girls' access to education around the world is Malala. In fact, I probably don't even have to tell you her surname (it's Yousafzai) because most of us know her by her given name. Born and raised in Pakistan, Malala first became known internationally in 2009, when she began writing a blog for the BBC about her life under Taliban rule. On October 9, 2012, Malala was shot at close range by the Taliban while taking a van home from school. She was hospitalized first in Pakistan and later in the United Kingdom. In 2014, at the age of seventeen, Malala became the youngest person in history to win the Nobel Peace Prize. In Malala's bestselling book, *I Am Malala: The Girl Who Stood Up for Education and Was Shot by the Taliban*, she asks, "If one man can destroy everything, why can't one girl change it?" If you want to know more about Malala, you can also watch the documentary *He Named Me Malala*.

## MARK YOUR CALENDARS, FEMINISTS!

July 12 is Malala's birthday. It also marks the day in 2013 on which Malala addressed the United Nations on the importance of girls' right to education. On that day in 2013 the United Nations declared July 12 Malala Day. The day reminds us to think of Malala and the millions of girls for whom access to education is limited or impossible. In her speech to the UN Youth Assembly, Malala said, "Malala Day is not my day. Today is the day of every woman, every boy and every girl who have raised their voice for their rights."

# ACCESS TO HEALTH CARE

Like access to education, access to health care is something many of us in the developed world take for granted. In Canada, a national health care system called Medicare means that citizens do not have to pay out of pocket for most medical services. The United States has a mixed public-private health system.

In many parts of the world, adequate health care is an unaffordable luxury. In addition to dealing with illnesses that affect all sexes, girls and women have specific reproductive-health issues.

The term **human rights** refers to things we are entitled to because we are human—and how we can expect to be treated. Access to health care is a basic human right.

When I started researching this chapter, I knew what **maternal mortality** meant: women who died during pregnancy and childbirth. But I had to look up the meaning of **maternal morbidity**. The term refers to any health condition attributed to or worsened by pregnancy and childbirth.

According to the United Nations Office of the High Commissioner for Human Rights information series on sexual and reproductive health and rights, in 2013 some 289,000 women died during or immediately following pregnancy and childbirth. That comes to an average of approximately 800 women a day. Ninety-nine percent of all maternal deaths occur in developing countries.

The main causes of maternal mortality are serious bleeding, infection and unsafe abortion—all of which are preventable if women have access to adequate health care. And young adolescents face a higher risk of complications and death as a result of pregnancy than older women do.

A worker from Marie Stopes International visits a community in Afghanistan to educate women about family planning.

Here's one more statistic to put things in perspective, this one from the World Health Organization. In 2013 the maternal mortality rate in developing countries was 230 per 100,000 live births. In developed nations, the rate was 16 per 100,000 live births.

Unsafe abortions can lead to severe injury and sometimes death. Access to safe and legal abortion is a vital right for all women.

Yet there are countries, such as Malta, the Dominican Republic, El Salvador, Nicaragua and Chile, where abortion is not allowed under any circumstances. In other countries, abortion is only permitted if a woman's life is in danger. In these countries, as well as in countries where abortion is prohibited altogether, women who wish to terminate their pregnancies often end up seeking illegal abortions. According to the World Health Organization, 25 million unsafe abortions are performed every year.

Here's the bottom line. Girls who attend school are less likely to become pregnant than girls who are not in school. They tend to have better self-esteem and more knowledge about birth control,

## THINKING OUTSIDE THE BOX

If we want to increase access to education for girls (as well as boys) in developing countries, we need to come up with innovative solutions. School-in-a-Box is a portable classroom designed for use in remote locations or in areas where it is too dangerous for children to get to school. Launched in 1995 in Rwanda by UNICEF, School-in-a-Box consists of an aluminum container filled with school supplies and materials for as many as 40 students. The lid of the box can be used as a blackboard.

and are more likely to resist violence. But if a young woman becomes pregnant and wishes to terminate the pregnancy, she should be able to have a safe abortion. If she chooses to have a baby, she should not have to fear illness—or, worse, death.

Sex education, which needs to include open, informed discussion about contraception, is an important way to help girls and women take charge of their reproductive health. We need to ensure that young people around the world are getting this kind of information.

There is some good news. Organizations around the world are working to support women's reproductive health. One is Marie Stopes International (MSI), a British **nongovernmental organization (NGO)** with offices in the United States and Australia. MSI works in thirty-seven countries to educate girls and women about pregnancy and help them get access to safe abortions. Founded in 1976, the organization's motto is "We help women to have children by choice, not chance." For more information about abortion rights, have a look at *My Body My Choice: The Fight for Abortion Rights* by Robin Stevenson (also in the Orca Issues series).

# FEMALE GENITAL MUTILATION

In 2012 the United Nations General Assembly adopted a resolution to ban a practice known as female genital mutilation (FGM). It refers to surgery performed on young girls (between infancy and adolescence) and sometimes on adult women. According to the World Health Organization, more than 200 million girls and women have been cut, in thirty countries in Africa, the Middle East and Asia, regions where FGM is most common.

The most common form of FGM is a procedure called a *clitoridectomy*, which refers to the total or partial removal of the clitoris, the small, sensitive, erectile part of the female genitals. There are no health benefits associated with FGM. In fact, FGM can cause serious complications. Short-term ones include heavy bleeding, severe pain, shock and sometimes death. Long-term consequences include vaginal, menstrual and urinary tract problems, as well as pain and decreased pleasure during sexual intercourse.

The latter, of course, is the whole idea. The procedure aims to ensure virginity before marriage, as well as fidelity during marriage. A woman without a clitoris is unlikely to have an orgasm. If sex is less than satisfying (or not satisfying at all), a woman may not seek a lover. If she is married, she will probably experience pain during sexual intercourse. Only the man's pleasure matters. Not only is the husband entitled to sexual pleasure, but he should not have to worry about his wife's sexual needs—or whether she will cheat on him.

I'm sure you can see what is wrong with this picture.

Despite the United Nations resolution, FGM remains the social norm in some countries. In fact, in these countries FGM

At the age of five Waris Dirie was subjected to female genital mutilation. Dirie became a supermodel and human rights activist. She is a vocal opponent of FGM and founder of the Desert Flower Foundation. .

is so widespread that it goes unquestioned, and there is societal pressure to conform.

Sex is not only about reproduction. Sex is a source of pleasure and intimacy. The ability to have and enjoy our sexuality is another basic human right.

The first step toward eliminating FGM is to talk openly about the topic. Many of the girls and women who have undergone FGM are reluctant to share their stories. Not Somali model, actress and author Waris Dirie, who is the world's best-known activist against FGM. Dirie was five when she underwent FGM. She shared her story in her 1998 autobiography *Desert Flower*, which went on to become a bestseller and later a movie. In 1997 Dirie was appointed the United Nations Special Ambassador for the Elimination of Female Genital Mutilation. She is also the founder of the Desert Flower Foundation, an organization that campaigns against FGM.

This Eritrean mother was pregnant with her son when the boat they were on overturned. They were detained in Libya for months. In this photo they are on their way to Niger thanks to the United Nations High Commissioner for Refugees (UNHCR, or United Nations Refugee Agency).

## WAR AND ITS EFFECTS ON GIRLS AND WOMEN

Gender-based inequality gets worse during armed conflict.

Violence to girls and women during wartime includes rape and sexual slavery. In 2008 the United Nations formally declared rape to be a "weapon of war."

In the past the main targets during war were soldiers, who were mostly male. Today, civilians—especially girls and women—have become primary targets. The abuse and rape of girls and women serve as a way to terrorize a community. When the local population cannot prevent the abuse of its girls and women, locals lose confidence in their leaders. According to UNICEF, in Rwanda between April 1994 and April 1995, more than 15,700 girls and women were raped.

Sadly, the arrival of peacekeeping troops does not always protect vulnerable girls and women. For instance, in Mozambique in 1992, after the signing of a peace treaty, United Nations Observer Mission soldiers recruited girls aged twelve to eighteen into prostitution.

In May 2015 in South Sudan, militia fighters attacked villages in the former state of Unity, beating and raping girls and women.

One woman interviewed by Human Rights Watch said that, to her, rape had become "just a normal thing." Militia fighters also kidnapped girls and women for use as "wives." Others were forced to work for the fighters—and were beaten as they worked.

One hundred thousand people fled Unity for a United Nations camp near Bentiu in South Sudan. But even there, girls and women faced tremendous danger. Those who fetched water or used the latrines at night were at an increased risk of violence and rape.

UNHCR, the United Nations Refugee Agency, is an organization working in over 130 countries to help people, including girls and women, who have been forced to flee their homes because of violence, persecution, war or disaster. UNHCR works to ensure that everybody has the right to seek asylum and find safe refuge. Besides providing on-the-ground life-saving emergency assistance, UNHCR helps build better futures for millions of people forced from home. UNHCR has a website with vital information for refugees and those who are assisting them. Established in 1950, UNHCR is funded by voluntary contributions, mostly from governments but also companies and the general public. UNHCR's Nobody Left Outside campaign has helped some two million people who have been forced to flee their homes.

In 2015 Yusra Mardini fled Syria. She was part of a group of refugees traveling from Turkey to Greece on a dinghy when it began to sink. Mardini swam alongside the boat for hours to lead it to shore. In 2016 she competed in the Rio de Janeiro Summer Olympics in swimming.

UNHCR provides information about which countries are willing to host refugees and also about initiatives such as the humanitarian corridors program, which recently made it possible for Barwako, a twelve-year-old Somali girl with a debilitating skin condition, to relocate to Italy, where she will finally get the medical treatment she needs.

# SEX SLAVERY

According to the United Nations, some 2.5 million people are ensnared in sex slavery, most of them girls and women.

*Sex slavery* is also known as *sex trafficking*—the term *trafficking* refers to the fact that victims are kidnapped, taken across national or international borders and forced to work as prostitutes. Transporting victims to countries where they cannot speak the language and have no friends reduces their ability to escape.

Sex slavery is often controlled by gangsters. They prey on the most vulnerable women—the poor, the uneducated and the isolated. Often girls are lured with the promise of a better life and legitimate work. But instead of getting a job in, for instance, a fruit stall or a café, they are taken to a brothel. If they refuse to have sex with clients, the girls are beaten and drugged. They are seldom paid for their work. And they are told that if they wish to leave, they will have to pay an exorbitant sum of money—an amount they will never be able to come up with.

In their book *Half the Sky: Turning Oppression into Opportunity for Women Worldwide*, Pulitzer Prize-winning journalists Nicholas D. Kristof and Sheryl WuDunn write movingly about the oppression of women. They point out that the countries with "the most straitlaced and sexually conservative societies," such as India, Pakistan and Iran, have the largest number of forced prostitutes. Since young men cannot have sex with their girlfriends, it is acceptable for them to have sex with prostitutes.

Kristof and WuDunn have visited brothels around the world. They have observed that "an essential part of the brothel business model is to break the spirit of girls through humiliation, rape, threats, and violence."

In May 2017, twenty-one members of an international sex-trafficking ring were arrested and charged. They had forced hundreds of Thai women to travel to the United States to work as sex slaves.

As for the children who are forced into sex trafficking, they are inevitably the most vulnerable members of our society, lacking the family support that many of us take for granted. In the United States, depending on the state, 50 to 80 percent of child sex-traffic victims have been involved in the child-welfare system.

For individuals who are forced into sex slavery, sex is not a source of pleasure or intimacy. Instead it is a transaction—and often a brutal one. We need to do everything we can to help girls and women who have been or are at risk of being forced into sex slavery.

In their book, Kristof and WuDunn describe how they have rescued girls and women from brothels. The couple inspired an organization, Half the Sky Movement (halftheskymovement.org), which uses a variety of multimedia tools to fight sex slavery and other injustices.

If your school is organizing a fundraising activity, consider donating the proceeds to an organization such as this one. Kristof and WuDunn believe it should be part of the North American university curriculum for students to travel and do community work in developing countries.

# Chapter Three

# MIRROR, MIRROR, ON THE WALL: THE FEMALE FOCUS ON APPEARANCE

n the fairy tale *Snow White*, the Evil Queen stands before her mirror and asks, "Mirror, mirror, on the wall, who is the fairest of them all?"

More than anything else, the Evil Queen wants to be the fairest—an old-fashioned word for the most beautiful. Notice that the Queen doesn't ask whether she is the kindest, smartest, most musical, best at math, funniest, or most astute politician in her kingdom. She has only one thing on her mind—her appearance.

The Evil Queen is reassured when the mirror tells her that she is indeed the most beautiful. But that reassurance does not last. Every day the Evil Queen poses the same question to her mirror. Perhaps she suspects something we all know—that external beauty does not last. When one day the mirror tells her that Snow White has surpassed her in terms of beauty, the Evil Queen is incensed.

Like many fairy tales, *Snow White* prompts us to think about important topics. Why, for instance, does appearance matter so much to girls and women?

The focus on female appearance begins almost as soon as we are born. The first compliment many people pay to little girls often has to do with their appearance ("You're so beautiful!" "I've never seen such long eyelashes!" "That is the prettiest dress!"). We are far less likely to praise a boy for his appearance.

Small wonder that girls grow up caring too much about how they look—and arguably too little about other areas of their lives. After all, looking good takes up a lot of time and costs a lot of money.

Conventional and social media contribute to the problem by presenting girls and women with impossibly high standards of beauty. Advertising also plays a huge part in making us feel bad about our bodies. Taken to an extreme, the obsession with *body image* can contribute to eating disorders like anorexia and bulimia. Striving to be "the fairest of them all" also breaks down bonds between women—weakening our power.

What, you may be asking, does any of this have to do with feminism?

The answer is, a lot.

There is nothing wrong with wanting to look good, but when we focus too much on our appearance, we have less time and energy to spend on other pursuits—such as our careers and the contributions we might make to society.

Every girl or woman I know has her own story of struggling with the pressure to be attractive. Here's mine.

When I was growing up, my mother would sometimes look at me and say, "Mo, you're having a beautiful day!" And all that day I would feel more special, like I really was beautiful. My mother was giving me the message that many mothers give daughters: we are valued for our attractiveness.

Fast forward to ninth grade. It was the 1970s, and straight hair was all the rage. Which meant my very curly hair was a problem. To make matters worse, my sister, Carolyn, who is two years younger than me, has perfectly straight hair that never gets frizzy.

For too long, Carolyn and I were rivals—not only about who was the smartest sister, but also about who was the most popular and, of course, the prettiest. Rivalries like ours are an unfortunate example of how competitiveness breaks down the bonds between women.

Every morning before school I begged Carolyn to blow-dry my hair—but she often refused (to be fair, it takes a long time to straighten hair as curly as mine), and I had to go to school with the frizzy, curly hair that I despised.

On to eleventh grade and a memory that's especially clear—and disturbing. It's a summer afternoon in Montreal, and I am in the backyard with my dad. "It looks like you have a spare tire around your belly," he tells me.

A 1977 photograph of the author with blow-dried hair. As a teenager she hated her curly hair.

That observation led me to go on a diet and begin exercising. By fall I had lost a lot of weight. Though my weight has been fairly consistent ever since, I have never stopped feeling self-conscious about my belly—and I rarely go a day without exercising.

Though my father did not mean to cause lifelong harm, he did. I still inspect myself critically every time I look into a mirror. When I meet other women, I automatically compare myself to them. When I get together with my female friends, we often critique other women's appearance. When I meet a girl baby, I often catch myself remarking on her looks.

I am working hard to change those old habits. Like many girls and women I need to keep reminding myself that appearance is only a small part of who we are. Focusing too much on how we look is a waste of time, energy and money. Perhaps if we begin by being more accepting of our physical selves, we will be more accepting of others.

We also need to stand up and protest when marketing campaigns aim to make us feel bad about ourselves. In 2014 three British women, Frances Black, Gabriella Kountourides and Laura Ferris, joined forces to protest a Victoria's Secret ad that depicted underwear-clad models next to the slogan "The Perfect Body." The three women started a Change.org petition in which they pointed out that women are "bombarded with advertisements aimed at making them feel insecure about their bodies, in the hope that they will spend money on products that will supposedly make them happier and more beautiful."

Victoria's Secret changed its advertisements when women objected to a slogan that made them feel insecure about their bodies.

More than 33,000 people signed the petition! And just so you know that protest can work—in response to the petition, Victoria's Secret changed its slogan to "A Body for Every Body."

I hope that after you read this chapter, you, too, will reevaluate what appearance means to you. Let's be more accepting of our own bodies, and the bodies of others, so that we can turn our attention to more important matters, such as making this world a better place.

## NO ONE LOOKS LIKE BARBIE!

If a real woman had a waist as tiny as the popular doll's, and breasts as large, she'd have difficulty walking. And those tiny, misshapen feet (caused, no doubt, by always wearing high heels) would cause serious lower back trouble. Yet since 1959, when the first Barbie doll appeared at the North American International Toy Fair in New York (wearing a black-and-white bathing suit), girls have wanted to look like Barbie. Most people don't know that Barbie was invented by a woman—Ruth Handler—who owned the Mattel company with her husband, Elliot.

For years feminists have been complaining about Barbie, which may be why, in 2015, Mattel changed its advertising approach and introduced Barbies who can wear flat shoes. The company also started to produce Barbies in eight different skin tones. In Mattel's 2015 ad, girls imagine themselves in professions such as veterinarian, soccer coach and university professor. *You can be anything*, the commercial proclaimed. Was this just a clever marketing strategy or a genuine acknowledgment that girls need to focus on more than appearance? The answer, probably, is a bit of both. To mark Women's Day 2018, Mattel launched its Inspiring Women Series. The first three dolls in the series pay tribute to Amelia Earhart, the first female aviator to fly across the Atlantic Ocean; Katherine Johnson, an African American mathematician who did important work at NASA; and Mexican artist and activist Frida Kahlo.

BEFORE AFTER

BEFORE AFTER

## SECONDHAND DOLLS GET THE ULTIMATE MAKEOVER

When Sonia Singh began upcycling discarded dolls in 2014, she was not trying to make a statement about feminism. "I just wanted to make the dolls look like the dolls I wanted to play with when I was a child," said Singh, who I interviewed by Skype from her home in Hobart, Tasmania. A former microbiologist and science educator, Singh, who is now 38, got into doll making when she was downsized. Little did she know her Tree Change Dolls would become an Internet sensation!

Singh finds most of her dolls at thrift shops and garage sales. Once she gets them home, she uses nail-polish remover to take off their makeup. She also restyles their hair to make it look more natural. She molds new feet for some of the dolls and gives them sensible footwear. Singh's mom, Silvia, pitches in by knitting clothes for the dolls.

"I don't pretty my dolls up. I dress them in practical clothing. People say the dolls look so much happier now," said Singh. She is delighted that her dolls are getting people to talk about our culture's focus on beauty. "If what I've done does make the big toy companies rethink the way they market and style their dolls, that's not a bad thing."

Singh has made about 600 dolls since 2014. Each doll sells for about $200 US. Singh donates 10 percent of all sales to charities such as Plan International. But Singh is not only interested in making sales. She encourages kids to restyle their own dolls. All you need to get started is nail-polish remover, acrylic paint and a fine paintbrush. "It's empowering for kids to create mini versions of themselves," said Singh.

# OBJECTIFICATION

When a man sees and treats a woman primarily like an object, checking out her face and body, and usually stopping at her breasts—some girls call this the "elevator stare"—that is *objectification*. By definition, objectification suggests that the viewer does not take into account a woman's other attributes, such as her capacity for compassion, her intelligence, her sense of humor or her creativity. Perhaps even worse, many girls and women engage in self-objectification, seeing their bodies from an outsider's perspective.

When I was growing up, the expression "she turns heads" was sometimes used to describe a beautiful woman. It went without saying that the heads this beautiful woman turned belonged to men. When they are out in the world, young girls and women are used to getting male attention. Sometimes this attention can feel flattering; other times it can feel downright creepy, even threatening.

Nancy Friday opens her book *The Power of Beauty* with a startling and honest admission: "I am a woman who needs to be seen. I need it in a basic way, as in to breathe, to eat...I have sought out men's eyes, required their gazes as far back as I can remember."

Ask yourself and your female friends whether you, too, crave the male gaze. It's nice to be admired. But when we rely on someone else to make us feel attractive, we're giving away an awful lot of power.

Here's another question for you and your friends: What makes you beautiful to you? When you answer, try not to focus on your external appearance. What's beautiful about the person you are inside?

Look at this photo before and after it has been retouched in Photoshop!

## MEDIA AND ADVERTISING

There's little doubt that the media as well as **advertisers** contribute to girls' and women's excessive focus on appearance. Advertisers have a vested interest in making girls and women feel inadequate. When we compare ourselves unfavorably to the Photoshopped models we see online and in magazines, we are more likely to buy makeup, hair-care products and brand-name clothing and accessories.

We are bombarded by images of women who appear perfect. So what if hairdressers and makeup artists have spent hours making models look the way they do? So what if the images we see have been Photoshopped? We want to look like those women. And if buying a $25 tube of mascara or a $200 pair of jeans will make us look like a model, well, it's worth the investment. Isn't it?

According to a March 2017 article on *BuzzFeed*, the average American woman will spend a whopping $300,000 on makeup during her lifetime. If that isn't bad enough, consider, too, the amount of time girls and women spend on their appearance. If, as they say, time is also money, we are wasting a lot of it. According to the same *BuzzFeed* article, women in New York spend twenty-one minutes a day applying makeup. That number doesn't take into account doing their hair, choosing what to wear or removing their makeup.

## THERE'S MORE TO LIFE THAN PINK AND BLUE

*Boys & Girls* not *Boys* and *Girls*. In September 2017, British department-store chain John Lewis launched a range of gender-neutral children's clothes and eliminated its formerly separate *Boys* and *Girls* sections. Caroline Bettis, head of childrenswear at John Lewis, explained the company's thinking: "We do not want to reinforce gender stereotypes." The chain store consulted with Let Clothes Be Clothes, a British parents' group that has been asking retailers to rethink how they design and market children's clothing. Not everyone was happy about the changes at John Lewis. One parent tweeted: *My child is a boy and will be dressed as a boy...rugby tops, polo shirts, jeans.* Gender stereotypes run deep, and genuine change will require open discussion—and time.

## TAXED FOR BEING FEMALE

In both Canada and the United States, sanitary pads and tampons are taxed—adding to their already high cost. When 14-year-old Kiva asked a male friend to pick up some tampons for her, he told her he was shocked at how expensive they were. Kiva has observed how squeamish people get when the subject of menstruation comes up. "People say, 'TMI,' but I'm not shy to say I've got my period." She has also noticed how guys blame everything on a girl's period. "If a girl is in a bad mood, she must be PMSing. Even if a girl is on her period, they don't get to say that," she said.

# SOCIAL MEDIA

There are lots of good things about social media. It helps us access information quickly. It allows us to build and participate in online communities. And yet, as we have seen, it can be harmful to our self-esteem.

Social media isn't helping girls and women feel good about themselves. It's common for girls to post selfies on platforms like Facebook and Instagram. And most girls won't just post any old photograph of themselves. How many times have you heard a girl say, "Delete that photo now! I swear I'll kill you if you post it!"? According to Renee Engeln, a psychology professor at Northwestern University and author of *Beauty Sick: How the Cultural Obsession with Appearance Hurts Girls and Women*, women are far more likely than men to untag photographs because they

*Posting just the right selfie (and forbidding friends from posting images of us that we don't like) is a good example of our obsession with appearance.*

don't like how they look in them. Engeln also points to studies showing that the more time girls and women spend on social media, the less satisfied they are with their own appearance.

Next time you catch yourself surfing the Web and feeling inadequate, stop! Consider limiting the time you spend on social media. On the days you spend less time online, do you feel better about yourself? Make sure you and your friends are media literate. When you admire a photograph of a model or an actress, remind yourself how much time must have gone into making her look so good.

How we spend our time says a lot about who we are and what matters most to us.

Molly-Beth is unusual. That's because this 14-year-old feels good about her appearance.

## BODY IMAGE

Body image is a major area of concern for many girls and women. With the exception of girls who are so thin that it is problematic (and sometimes even then), almost every female student I have ever taught wishes she could lose weight. (I know because I raise the subject of body image in my classes.)

Engeln reveals that 34 percent of five-year-old girls engage in "deliberate dietary restraint at least 'sometimes'" and that 40 percent of girls between the ages of five and nine wish they were thinner.

Many girls' self-esteem drops sharply at puberty, when the body undergoes rapid changes. Girls who were once interested in playing sports and roughhousing begin to feel pressure to look a certain way and behave in ways that are considered more feminine. Many begin to compare themselves to other girls and often end up feeling dissatisfied with their own unique appearance.

## FAT IS NOT A FEELING!

"I feel fat!" How many times have you heard a girl or woman say that? Or maybe you have said it yourself. Psychologists believe that when girls and women use that line, it has little to do with their weight. Instead, psychologists suggest, girls and women say it to express other, more difficult-to-express feelings such as dissatisfaction with their lives, a sense of loss or lack of fulfillment. Next time you catch yourself saying, "I feel fat," stop and ask yourself whether there is a deeper feeling you might be ignoring.

Most pubescent boys, on the other hand, think they look just fine. In fact, Engeln points out, most boys' satisfaction with their bodies improves once they hit puberty.

Nancy Friday describes the drop in girls' self-esteem that occurs at puberty as a "negative makeover." She believes the problem is connected to society's reluctance to talk about menstruation, which is, after all, a natural and healthy part of female life. Other researchers point out that, for girls, the changes that occur at puberty are often associated with weight gain, leaving many of them even unhappier about their bodies than they were before.

Fourteen-year-old Molly-Beth is an exception—she feels good about who she is and how she looks. "I don't feel pressure to look good," she told me. But Molly-Beth, who is going into ninth grade, says she is accustomed to hearing other girls complain that they feel fat. "I look at them and either they're skinny or they look perfectly fine," Molly-Beth says.

For Molly-Beth, being healthy matters more than looking good. She thinks that for her, attending an all-girls school and having a mom who is a strong role model have helped her stay focused on learning. "I'd like to be a lawyer. My favorite subject is English. I love reading and journaling," she says.

Engeln reports that girls as young as eleven are developing eating disorders like anorexia and bulimia. Though boys and men may develop eating disorders, they are far more prevalent in girls and women. "If," writes Engeln, "you heard that a young person was suffering from anorexia or bulimia and guessed it was a young woman, you'd be right nine times out of ten."

Even when they become dangerously thin, individuals who suffer from anorexia or bulimia often continue to see themselves as overweight when they look in the mirror. They suffer from what psychologists call **body image distortion** or **body dysmorphic disorder**. Sometimes they become so undernourished that hospitalization is required. Treatment is not always effective, and some anorexics and bulimics die as a result of their illnesses.

It's not easy to admit you are or have been anorexic. Despite the prevalence of eating disorders, we tend to have a negative opinion of individuals who suffer from them—as if having an eating disorder is their own fault. But we also tend to compliment girls and women who are very thin. Eating disorders are complex and can take years to treat.

Maria, now thirty-three, is my former student. She developed anorexia when she was in high school. "I had been a perfectionist until grade six. After grade six I put academics aside. I was overweight and trying to focus on developing a social life, which never worked because I never felt like I belonged. Then in grades ten and eleven my perfectionism came back. I started to apply perfectionism to my eating. I was always a chunky kid. Between October and March I lost a lot of weight. I ended up losing hair. I was very pale and iron-deficient."

Maria credits her high school English teacher with getting her back on track. "She spoke to me," Maria recalls. "My teacher caring about me when I didn't care about myself—that's what turned me around. Another big factor was my love for my mom. I saw how concerned she was about my weight loss and my health, and I didn't want to keep putting her through that."

Maria turned to school counselors at her high school, and later at college and university, for support. At university, Maria wrote her master's thesis on the subject of eating-disorders prevention in schools. Looking back, she wishes she had gone sooner and on a regular basis to see a psychologist who specialized in treating eating disorders. Even now that Maria is healthy, she says, "Recovery is a day-by-day process." She believes schools need to play an active role in supporting students' wellness. "Girls with a propensity to developing eating disorders or who have eating disorders are often not even aware of their symptoms."

## PERIOD STAINS ARE PART OF LIFE!

In 2015 Toronto, Ontario, poet Rupi Kaur posted a photo on Instagram of a woman lying in bed. No big deal, right? Wrong! That's because period stains were visible on the photograph—one on the woman's sweatpants, another on the sheets. Alerted by a viewer who complained about the photograph, Instagram removed the photo—twice. Kaur received a note that read *We removed your post because it doesn't follow Community Guidelines.*

It turns out, however, that Instagram's guidelines don't actually mention period stains. Instagram prohibits nudity, sexual acts and violence. Kaur moved the photo to Facebook, where she wrote, *Thank you Instagram for providing me with the exact response my work was created to critique.* Eventually Instagram restored the photo. But Kaur had made her point. Period stains—like menstruation itself—are a natural and normal part of our experience as women.

This model wears a shirt from the Drop the Label Movement. Founded in Phoenix, AZ, in 2016 by a mother and daughter, Drop the Label is a response to the tyranny and arbitrariness of size labels on women's clothing. The movement also fights fat phobia and raises awareness about eating disorders.

## MAKING COMPARISONS

Constantly comparing ourselves to other girls and women is not only depressing, but it also creates a sense of competitiveness, which can break down bonds of friendship. Have you ever met another girl or woman and immediately started comparing yourself to her or criticizing her? *I wish I had long legs like hers!* or *She'd be so much prettier if she lost ten pounds!*

Other girls and women need our support, not our criticisms of their appearance.

More and more girls and women are standing up to a phenomenon called **body shaming**. We've all heard or read about women who mock or humiliate other women based on their body shape or size.

We need to change those behaviors and our underlying attitudes if we want to put an end to body shaming. A social media
platform called Odyssey offers useful tips to get us started.
Odyssey points out that girls and women
are not only shamed for being fat; they are
also shamed for being skinny. Here's one
of Odyssey's tips: "Don't tell thin women
to eat a cheeseburger. Don't tell fat women
to put down their forks."

Odyssey also reminds us not to jump
to conclusions. A heavier person may
be struggling with a thyroid disorder.
Someone thinner may be recovering from
an eating disorder. Basing someone's worth
(including our own) strictly on appearance
is just plain wrong.

Engeln proposes a simple solution.
Instead of focusing on what our bodies
*look like*, she suggests we focus instead on
what our bodies can *do*.

*Girls and women are working together to end body
shaming and fight the cultural obsession with thinness.
This image is from a series of photos by Jess Fielder.*

Consider how you walk up and down
stairs, how your body digests food, how
your heart pumps blood to your lungs and then to the rest of
your body, how your brain learns new things. Pretty amazing,
don't you agree?

Strong girls and women don't just have strong bodies.

We have strong minds and spirits.

And we know that there is a lot more to life than how we look.

I CHOOSE YOU

NO MEANS NO

I DO

I DON'T

BE MINE

DON'T HIT ME

*Chapter Four*

# FEMINISTS IN LOVE: NAVIGATING THE WORLD OF SEX AND ROMANCE

When I was growing up in the 1960s, one of the most popular schoolyard songs went like this: "X (insert a girl's name) and Y (insert a boy's name) sitting in a tree, K-I-S-S-I-N-G (spell out each letter). First comes love, then comes marriage, then comes a baby in a baby carriage."

For many women of my generation, getting married and having children (in that order) were at the top of our to-do list. I remember that my mom had two single female friends—and that we always felt a little sorry for them.

As little girls growing up in the 1960s, my friends and I often "played house." We'd pretend to be wives and mothers with devoted, hardworking husbands and well-behaved children. We'd also discuss the names we would give to the children we would have one day.

For most of today's girls and women, marriage and having children are simply options. While some young women still long for old-fashioned romance, others are more interested in casual,

Even in today's world, many young women have an idealized view of romantic relationships. Some still dream about meeting Prince or Princess Charming, who will make their lives perfect.

less committed sexual relationships. Still other girls and women are happily single. And, of course, our views and desires can change over time. Our life situations will change too. A breakup may leave us single. Someone who planned on remaining single may find herself falling in love and wanting to plan a future with her boyfriend or girlfriend.

The point is—we have choices. There are many ways to be happy. And that's a good thing!

But even with so many options to choose from, many girls and women still feel pressure to be in a "relationship." Take all the hype, for example, around Valentine's Day. If we don't get a Hallmark card or flowers or a heart-shaped box of chocolates, well, then, something must be wrong with us!

There is even a term for the assumption that we should be part of a couple: *amatonormativity*. Coined by Arizona State University philosophy professor Elizabeth Brake, the term plays on the word *heteronormativity*, which is a viewpoint that sees heterosexuality as a given instead of one of many possibilities. Amatonormativity refers to society's obsession with romantic, sexual love. *Haven't you met anyone yet? What do you mean, you don't have a boyfriend or girlfriend?*

Gender plays a role here too. Girls and women face more pressure to be in a relationship than boys and men do. A single man is a fun-loving bachelor (there's nothing negative about that term), whereas a single woman is a spinster or an old maid, negative terms that suggest a single woman is lonely and unable to attract a partner for romance and sex.

In an article published on *Healthyway*, Brooke Geller looked at amatonormativity. Geller observed that "there's so much value placed on being in a relationship that it's often regarded as the only true way to feel complete." But she also pointed out that being single can bring important discoveries: it's "an opportunity to get to know yourself and grow as a person."

Like most young people, fifteen-year-old Emmy knows the statistics about divorce—that four out of ten marriages fail. Even so, Emmy still believes in the possibility of a storybook romance. "I believe there is a Prince Charming, but I haven't met him yet," she says. Emmy can even describe her Prince Charming, and she says she'd rather wait for him than settle for someone else. "He'd be," she says, "the male equivalent of me—someone who likes kids, reading, playing music and being with family and friends."

Evvie, who is also fifteen, is looking for something different when it comes to relationships. "At our age, it's not like we're going to end up marrying any guy we go out with. I'd rather just hook up."

*Hookup* is the term used to refer to casual sexual encounters without emotional bonds or long-term commitments. According to the American Psychological Association, 60 to 80 percent of North American college students have had some sort of hookup experience.

For some women, hookups are a way to have "strings-free" sex.

There's nothing wrong with hooking up—as long as women are not having sex because they feel pressured by their partners. This raises an important issue: **consent**.

Then there is the question of the **sexual double standard**. Just as single women have tended to be seen as objects of pity ("spinsters" and "old maids"), women who have had many sexual partners are perceived very differently than men who have had many sexual partners.

In this chapter we'll also talk about another unfortunate reality—**date rape**. While it is true that some girls and women are raped by strangers, most rapes are perpetrated by boys and men that we know.

## BAD BOYS, BAD BOYS

What is it about bad boys? Later in this book you'll read about a feminism club that meets once a week at Royal West Academy in Montreal. The club is run by Bronwyn, 15, and Esme, 16. Both young women have lots to say about romantic relationships.

"I believe in true love," said Bronwyn. Then she added, "I've had crushes on the worst people." Bronwyn has given a lot of thought to why girls might be attracted to bad boys. "When I was little, I was told if boys are mean to you, they like you. And sometimes women look for bad boys so they can fix them," she said.

Esme describes herself as "afraid of love." Her fear is the result of a two-month-long relationship she had at 15. "He was controlling and constantly angry at me. He didn't want me talking to other people. He was even jealous of my projects. He threatened to kill himself if we broke up," she said.

Then there are the girls and women who fall in love with partners who are abusive—emotionally, physically or both. One of the reasons it is not always easy for girls and women to leave abusive relationships is that they are afraid to be alone. This fear of being alone is connected to the pressure many girls and women feel to be in a relationship. *My partner may not be perfect. But if I break up with him (or her), how will I ever find someone else?*

In this chapter we will also examine the institution of marriage. Perhaps if marriage were a more equitable institution—if, for example, partners divided home and childcare responsibilities equally—divorce would be less common.

# CONSENT

Lately we've been hearing—and talking—a lot about the issue of consent. You should never engage in sexual activities unless you want to and are able to give clear verbal consent. In order to avoid sexual diseases and unwanted pregnancy, contraception (and condoms) should be nonnegotiable.

Recent allegations against American actor and comedian Aziz Ansari—best known for being the creator and star of the Netflix series *Master of None*—demonstrate the importance of clear verbal consent.

In January 2018 an anonymous woman published her account of a date with Ansari, describing it as "the worst night of my life." Using the pseudonym Grace, the woman recalled going back to Ansari's apartment but "feeling uncomfortable at how quickly things escalated."

In a statement following the allegations, Ansari said the encounter was "by all indications completely consensual."

Was this simply a matter of *he said, she said?* Lots of people had lots to say after the allegations surfaced. Many criticized Grace for not having been more clear. Why, they asked, did she go back to Ansari's apartment in the first place, and why didn't she simply leave when she began to feel uncomfortable? Others, including Jessica Valenti, objected to the fact that Grace was being blamed for what had happened. They used the incident to emphasize the urgent

imagine if men were as disgusted with rape as they are with periods

We hide our sanitary napkins and tampons in the bottoms of our purses and backpacks. Many boys and men get squeamish if someone mentions periods. But they often fail to object when someone makes a rape joke.

need to discuss sexual respect and clear consent. As Valenti wrote in a tweet, *This is why "yes means yes" models of consent are so necessary.*

The use and overuse of alcohol and drugs also need to be part of the discussion about consent. Many rape cases involve survivors who are drunk or stoned. Few of these survivors go to the police, largely out of fear they will be blamed for what happened. But if a person is too inebriated to give clear verbal consent, that means she (or he) has not agreed to engaging in sexual activities.

Unfortunately, the courts do not always support this view. In 2017 Nova Scotia provincial court judge Gregory Lenehan acquitted a Halifax taxi driver of sexual assault. In his ruling, Lenehan said, "Clearly, a drunk can consent."

Lenehan's decision led to a public outcry. In September 2017 Nova Scotia's chief justice set up a review committee to investigate allegations of misconduct against Lenehan. In April 2018 the review committee found that Lenehan had committed no misconduct in acquitting the taxi driver.

If we want to ensure that girls and women are not having sex because they feel pressured to do so, we need to talk openly and a lot about consent. The term *enthusiastic consent* has been gaining popularity. It suggests that mere consent is not enough—that a person who has agreed to have sex should be as into it as her (or his) partner.

Founded in 2001 in British Columbia by the Victoria Sexual Assault Centre, Project Respect aims to educate young people about consent, urging them to "join the respect revolution." Its website lays out the philosophy that "positive sexuality begins with enthusiastic consent." Project Respect provides posters to schools and offers educational workshops and leadership training for all genders of youth in middle schools, high schools, community programs and conferences. People in crisis can access VSAC's Sexual Assault Response Team by calling the Vancouver Island Crisis Line at 1-888-494-3888 and they will be re-directed. Access to non-emergency services can be done through calling their Service Access Line at 250-383-3232.

# THE SEXUAL DOUBLE STANDARD

The term *sexual double standard* refers to society's vastly different attitude toward sexually active males and females. Sexually active males are generally perceived as players—macho and cool. Society's view of sexually active females isn't nearly so positive. Consider, for example, the word *slut*. It is commonly used to describe a girl or woman who is sexually active. Don't you find it interesting that men get points for being sexually active while sexually active women get insulted?

The term **slut shaming** is used to describe how females are labeled and punished for being sexually active. Leora Tanenbaum's

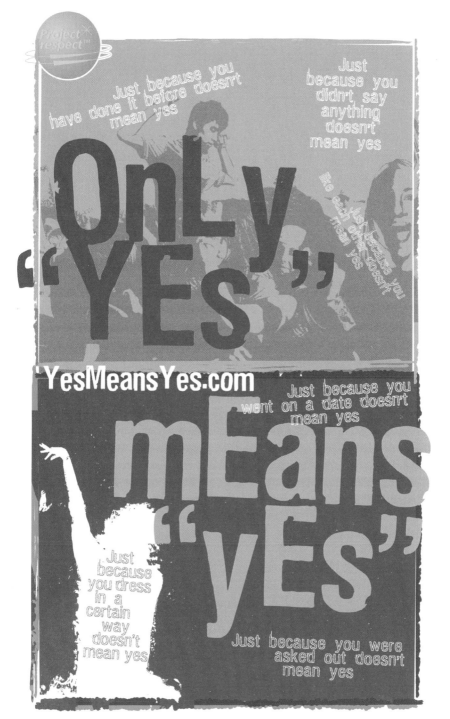

An Initiative of the Victoria Women's Sexual Assault Centre

Crisis and Info Line
(250) 383-3232

Funded by: Vancity, The Victoria Foundation, and the Province of British Columbia

book *I Am Not a Slut: Slut-Shaming in the Age of the Internet* is the result of more than twenty years of investigating slut shaming. Tanenbaum is concerned about how widespread and "normal" slut shaming is. As she wrote in a blog post for the *Huffington Post*, "Boys will be boys and girls will be sluts."

Tanenbaum points out that it is not uncommon for boys to take anonymous photographs of naked, unconscious girls and post them on Facebook. These kinds of slut-shaming acts can have traumatic results, including suicide. In 2012 Amanda Todd, a British Columbia teen, took her life after being bullied into exposing her breasts on webcam. In 2013 Rehtaeh Parsons committed suicide in her home in Nova Scotia. She'd allegedly been gang-raped at a party; one of her assailants later posted photos of her online. The photos went viral, and Rehtaeh was deluged by text messages from boys wanting to have sex with her, as well as from girls accusing her of being a slut.

By speaking publicly about Rehtaeh's experience, Leah Parsons, Rehtaeh's mother, is working to fight against slut shaming and bullying of all kinds. In an interview with the *Chronicle Herald* newspaper, Leah Parsons said, "Rehtaeh would want her story out there."

## DATE RAPE

You are a girl or woman walking home alone. It is dark, and a man approaches you from behind.

How do you feel?

Every girl or woman knows the answer to that question. Afraid. That is because we have all been there. In fact, even just writing those two sentences made my heart race!

While it is possible that a girl or woman may be raped by a stranger when she is walking alone at night, the truth is that most

RAPE HAPPENS TO WOMEN IN BURKAS AND STABLE RELATIONSHIPS.
CLOTHES ARE IRRELEVENT
RAPE IS NEVER DESERVED

Protesters march in Manchester, UK, in June 2011.

# #BEENRAPEDNEVERREPORTED

This Twitter hashtag went viral in the fall of 2014. It started as a Facebook conversation between two Canadian journalists who had never met in person, Sue Montgomery and Antonia Zerbisias. At the time Montgomery, now mayor of the Côte-des-Neiges–Notre-Dame-de-Grâce borough in Montreal, was working for the *Montreal Gazette*; Zerbisias wrote for the *Toronto Star*. Both women had been raped and had not reported the crimes. Montgomery was raped by her grandfather when she was a child, and later at age 21 by a colleague working at Air Canada. The two women were inspired to start the hashtag following news of alleged victims of well-known CBC personality Jian Ghomeshi.

Montgomery was on assignment, covering a murder trial at the Montreal Court House, when she sent out the first tweet with the hashtag #BeenRapedNeverReported. "I was afraid that Internet trolls would attack me, but nobody did. Then the tweets kept coming, one after the other. I was shaking. What, I wondered, had I unleashed?" she said to me.

Within 48 hours, 10 million people from around the world had taken part in #BeenRapedNeverReported. Perhaps because they were anonymous, women felt they could finally share their stories. "A lot of people were thanking me. They had never told anyone before that they had been raped. When you only have 140 characters, you don't have to go into a lot of detail. There's no need for your real name or for you to name the perpetrator," said Montgomery.

Here are two of the deeply moving tweets: "Because when you're young and no one really believes you anyway" and "Didn't know I could [report] because I was sixteen and he was my boyfriend."

After the hashtag went viral, Montgomery was interviewed by ICI Radio-Canada as well as the BBC. "We had lanced a boil. It's important for women to see they are not alone. They don't have to suffer in silence. We are creating a global conversation," said Montgomery.

girls and women are raped by someone they know—a relative, a friend, sometimes even a boyfriend or husband.

The facts are grim. According to SexAssault.ca, a website that provides information for Canadian victims of sexual abuse, most sexual assaults are committed by someone close to the victim, not a stranger. Eighty percent of assailants are friends and family of the victim. According to the same website, one in four North American women will be sexually assaulted during her lifetime. Seventeen percent of girls under the age of sixteen have experienced some form of incest. Eighty-three percent of disabled women will be sexually assaulted during their lifetimes. Fifty-seven percent of Indigenous women have been sexually assaulted. Only 6 in every 100 incidents of sexual assault are reported to the police.

Rape is one of the most underreported crimes. Victims of sexual assault fear they will not be believed—and might even be blamed. If a sexual assault goes to trial, victims may be questioned about their sexual history, how they were dressed at the time of the assault, whether they had been drinking or whether they may have given the assailant some sign that they were interested in having sex with him.

In her book *Full Frontal Feminism: A Young Woman's Guide to Why Feminism Matters*, Jessica Valenti challenges the tendency to blame sexual-assault victims. As Valenti puts it, "Women (and men) have to know that there is nothing you can do that warrants being raped…I don't care if you are a naked, drunk, passed-out prostitute."

When I was seventeen, a friend who was a year older than me told me she had been raped. She told me it had happened the previous weekend, after a party where she had had too much to drink—she accepted a ride home with a young man she didn't know well. I could see my friend was shaken up, but otherwise

## NAIL POLISH DOES DOUBLE DUTY

Four North Carolina State University engineering students have invented a nail polish that changes color if it comes in contact with date-rape drugs such as rohypnol and GHB. Produced by Undercover Colors, a nail-tech company, the nail polish hit the market in 2017. A girl or woman wearing the polish only has to dip a finger into her drink to see if it is spiked.

Though the product has gained international media attention, some rape-prevention activists have reservations about the new nail polish. They worry that it places responsibility on potential victims and could lead to more victim blaming: will girls or women be blamed for not wearing the polish? As Tracey Vitchers, chairperson of an organization called Students Active For Ending Rape, said in an interview with the online news site ThinkProgress: "I think we need to think critically about why we keep placing the responsibility for preventing sexual assault on young women."

## SPIKED DRINKS AND DATE-RAPE DRUGS

I first heard about Rohypnol (commonly called a roofie) from one of my students. Like ketamine and gamma-hydroxybutyrate (GHB), Rohypnol is a date-rape drug. Colorless, tasteless, odorless and illegal, it can be slipped into someone's drink. The effects of Rohypnol include loss of muscle control, confusion, drowsiness and amnesia. One of my students told me that her older sister had met a guy in a bar who offered to get her a drink. She couldn't remember much after that. Only that she woke up the following morning in the emergency room at Montreal's Royal Victoria Hospital. She had been raped, beaten and left for dead.

In September 2018 American actor and comedian Bill Cosby was sent to prison for the sexual assault of a woman in his home. Cosby will serve three to ten years for drugging and sexually assaulting Andrea Constand, a Temple University basketball team manager, in Philadelphia, Pennsylvania, in 2004. Dozens of other women also came forward to make similar allegations against Cosby. During Cosby's 2017 trial, prosecutors referred to a quote from his 1991 book *Childhood*, in which Cosby wrote that girls "are never in the mood for us. They need chemicals." Many people believe that the #MeToo campaign and Time's Up movement (you'll learn about them in chapter 5) affected the jury's decision to find Cosby guilty.

she seemed okay. I did not suggest she go to a doctor or to the police. As far as I know, she never told her parents about what had happened.

My friend left Montreal a few years after the assault. Recently we reconnected. She told me her life was marked by that incident so many years ago. In those days, no one used the term *date rape*. I wish I had known then about date rape. I wish I had been able to point my friend to resources that might have helped her cope. I wish she had gone to the police. We don't know what became of the young man. Had my friend reported the rape to the police, might other young women have been spared what happened to my friend?

# INTIMATE PARTNER VIOLENCE

I wish I didn't know so much about this subject.

Unfortunately I'm an expert on intimate partner violence.

I spent more than five years of my life with a boyfriend who beat me up. I was seventeen when we met and twenty-two when I finally left. I didn't tell anyone what was going on. When my boyfriend got angry, he always punched me in my right eye. I got accustomed to applying blue and purple eye shadow to the other eye in the hope that people wouldn't notice.

I spent most of those five years in a state of deep denial. Like many girls and women who stay in relationships where there is violence, I grew up with a parent who was also prone to violent outbursts. That may be one of the reasons it took me so long to leave my boyfriend.

I felt I was to blame for our problems. That if I tried harder, our relationship would improve. I was also afraid of living on my own—of not having a boyfriend.

When he threatened to kill me, I fled to a neighbor's apartment. That was the first time I saw the truth about my situation: I was a battered woman.

A few paragraphs back I wrote the line *Unfortunately I'm an expert on intimate partner violence.* But you know what? In many ways I now feel fortunate. Not to have been abused—nobody deserves that—but fortunate because I survived and made a good life for myself. My experience has also made it possible for me to connect with and maybe even be a role model to other girls and women who are or have been victims of intimate partner violence.

According to the World Health Organization, intimate partner violence is a major public health problem. The organization estimates that worldwide, one in three women has

In the HBO series Big Little Lies, Celeste Wright (played by Nicole Kidman) pretends to the world and to herself that her abusive husband is perfect.

experienced physical and/or sexual intimate partner violence. Thirty-eight percent of murders of women are committed by an intimate male partner.

Men can also be victims of intimate partner violence. According to Statistics Canada, men report being victims of spousal violence as frequently as women do. However, violence perpetrated by women against men tends to be far less severe and is less likely to involve sexual assault, beating, choking or gun- or knife-related threats. There is also same-sex intimate partner violence. According to the United States Centers for Disease Control and Prevention, 44 percent of gay women and 26 percent of gay men have been assaulted by a partner. Within the LGBTQ+ community, trans people and bisexual women face the highest rates of sexual violence.

Abuse—whether it is physical, sexual or emotional—rarely happens only once. It almost always escalates, becoming more frequent and intense. Counselors who work with abused girls and women describe a cycle of violence. First there is *tension*. Victims of intimate partner violence often use the expression "walking on eggshells" to describe what it feels like to be in this phase.

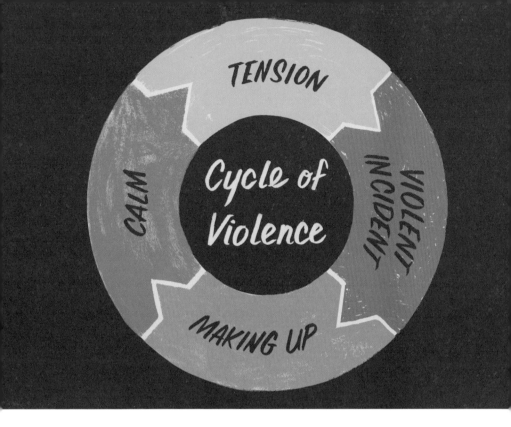

Their partner is in a bad mood and anything could set off his (or her) temper. Next comes the *violent incident*. The violent incident is followed by a period of *making up*. The abuser may apologize and promise never to hurt his partner again. He may buy her gifts. Making up is generally followed by a period of *calm*. Often the partner will act as if nothing bad ever happened.

But the calm does not last. It will almost inevitably be replaced by tension—and the cycle continues, on and on, until the abused partner finds the strength to get help and perhaps leave the relationship. If the violence continues to escalate, people die.

Many people think that only poor, uneducated women are victims of intimate partner violence. Although it's true that women with less privilege are at greater risk of physical and emotional violence, intimate partner violence is an epidemic that can strike any woman. It can be especially difficult for an educated, financially comfortable woman to admit she is the victim of intimate partner violence. Shouldn't a woman like that be able to leave her partner without looking back?

And, of course, some women are abused by wealthy, powerful partners. These women may fear the financial and social consequences of reporting on and leaving their spouses. In the prize-winning HBO series *Big Little Lies*, Nicole Kidman plays Celeste Wright, a former lawyer turned stay-at-home mom who is abused by her wealthy lawyer husband, Perry. Perry appears, at least on the surface, to be the perfect spouse, and his wife works hard to keep their secret.

But by discussing these topics openly, we can help to make change. If you or someone you know is the victim of intimate partner violence, get help. If you are in Canada, contact the Canadian Resource Centre for Victims of Violence. You can find the organization online or call them at 1-877-232-2610. If you are in the United States, contact the National Domestic Violence Hotline at 1-800-799-7233.

## BRUISES HEAL, SCARS REMAIN

The effects of intimate partner violence are long lasting. Here's what a woman I interviewed for the *Montreal Gazette* had to say about the long-term effects of intimate partner violence. She had left her abusive partner ten months earlier: "When I come to my apartment, even though he's not there, I'm afraid he is. Sometimes I lift the sheets to make sure he's not there." She is not alone. According to a longitudinal study carried out in Britain over a ten-year period and published in the journal *Depression and Anxiety* in 2015, the long-term effects of intimate partner violence include twice the likelihood of developing depression. Victims of intimate partner violence also have a three times higher risk of developing schizophrenia-like psychotic symptoms.

*Marriages in which spouses are true partners—each taking responsibility for chores and childcare—have a strong chance of success.*

## THE INSTITUTION OF MARRIAGE

With approximately 40 percent of North American marriages ending in divorce, there's a chance that if you have two parents, they are divorced. If they're not, you probably know other couples whose marriages have failed.

Arguing is normal and healthy. In fact, experts on marriage have identified the ability to deal with conflict as one of the most important signs of a healthy relationship.

Ideally, marriage is a partnership. While it is true that husbands now tend to do far more in terms of helping around the house and looking after children than husbands did a generation or two ago, wives today still do too much of the heavy lifting. According to an article published in 2015 in the *Wall Street Journal*, 41 percent of women who work outside the home do more childcare than their husbands, and 30 percent do more chores than their husbands.

Changing entrenched habits is not easy. In *ManifestA: Young Women, Feminism, and the Future*, authors Jennifer Baumgardner and Amy Richards warn that "it's behind the closed doors of families that equality can be hardest to find."

In 2006 the United States Department of Health and Human Services published a study called "The Importance of Fathers in the Healthy Development of Children." The study indicated that fathers are a lot more than simply the second adult in a family. It concludes that children whose fathers are actively involved in their lives have higher cognitive abilities and greater emotional well-being.

Research shows that kids whose fathers are actively involved in their lives do better at school, are less depressed, have better peer relations and experience less stress than kids whose fathers are less involved in their lives. There's more! Wives of husbands who are involved in their children's lives—that means changing diapers, picking up a child from the school nurse's office, doing carpool, helping with homework—have a greater sense of well-being than wives whose husbands leave these kinds of tasks to their spouses.

Many of us have become so used to the old pattern of women handling most of the chores and childcare that we are sometimes reluctant to give up the very chores we complain about! Men and women both need to work to make relationships more equitable and give them a greater chance of success.

*Chapter Five*

# NINE TO FIVE AND THEN SOME: THE FIGHT FOR EQUALITY IN THE WORKPLACE

Work is part of most people's lives, whether it's schoolwork, volunteer work, housework, a part-time job, a full-time job or, for many of us, some mix of all of these. With some exceptions (looking after our own children and homes and volunteer work), we are paid for the work we do. Our wages make it possible for us to pay for our living expenses and, if there is enough money left, to save and perhaps spend on things we value—which can be anything from contributing to causes we deem worthy to traveling to faraway places.

Of course, not everyone earns enough money to be able to save money or travel. Many people struggle to cover basic expenses. Women are particularly vulnerable to poverty. In her 2015 book *Unfinished Business: Women, Men, Work, Family*, Anne-Marie Slaughter shares a shocking statistic: "one in three adult women is living in poverty or just on the edge of poverty. For single mothers, the picture is particularly bleak."

Dollhouses like this one are being made increasingly gender neutral. It's a way of encouraging boys to play with something once seen as being only for girls.

If you are lucky, you will have enough money to live comfortably. If you are even luckier, you will enjoy the work you do, and your work, like your relationships, will allow you to become the kind of person you hope to be.

When I was growing up in the 1960s, only one of my friends' moms worked outside the home. Mrs. Munro was the school secretary. In our community, dads were the breadwinners. In fact, we rarely saw anybody's dad on a weekday. If a kid was running a fever and had to be picked up from the nurse's office, Mom would turn up.

In the 1940s, after nearly three years in a Nazi concentration camp, my own mother started but did not complete law school in Leiden, a city in the Netherlands. She didn't drop out. In fact, she was a top student. But her parents decided to move to the United States, and when she got there she never pursued her education.

Instead she married my dad, whom she had met in law school in the Netherlands, and they moved to Montreal. She worked as a secretary in order to cover her new husband's tuition at the Université de Montréal's Faculty of Law. It was a familiar story for her generation.

I don't think my mother was unhappy being a stay-at-home mom, but sometimes I wonder if she might have liked to explore other career possibilities. The daughter of a Dutch artist, she used to make gorgeous doodles. She was also a gifted storyteller. I inherited my love of stories from her. If circumstances had been different, and had she lived in a different time, might my mother have become a lawyer, an artist or an author?

When I was a little girl, I didn't only play house. I also played school in our basement, and I loved to write stories, but I never really imagined that I would have a career. I expected that, like my mom, I would have a husband who would go to work, and I would stay home and raise our children—and perhaps get an "allowance" on Friday nights the way my mom did.

A lot has changed. Not just for me, but for most girls and women.

When my first marriage ended I was in my mid-twenties, with only about twenty dollars to my name. But I also had a part-time job teaching composition at the local university, and I had just completed a master's degree in English literature. Luckily I was able to land a full-time teaching job at Marianopolis College, where I am still on the faculty. Teaching has provided financial security and brought me the satisfaction that comes from helping others. The writing came later. Though I never planned any of it, I'm glad things turned out the way they did.

Remember how I told you in chapter 2 that on the first day of school I always tell my students about the school I visited in Kenya and remind them how lucky they are to be studying in Canada? I also advise my students to find a career that can support them financially and that they enjoy, so that even those who decide to stay home and raise children can be financially independent should they ever need to be.

It would be wrongheaded to suggest that as young women make their way in the workplace they will not encounter obstacles having to do with their gender. There is still *pay inequity*. Certain professions remain male dominated. Many women still report that it is almost impossible to climb the ranks in their workplace due to a phenomenon referred to as the *glass ceiling*. And, of course, sexual harassment persists in many workplaces.

But there is good news too: more and more schools are doing their part to show today's girls that they really can be anything they want to be.

## PAY INEQUITY

Martine Bégin, a Quebecer who has been at the forefront of the province's pay-equity movement, gave me a powerful everyday example of pay inequity: "When we hire a babysitter—it's generally a girl—we pay her five dollars an hour and entrust her with our children. When we pay someone to shovel snow or mow our lawn—it's generally a boy—we usually pay ten dollars for a half hour's work. That's four times the pay. When adults do this, they're not aware that they're discriminating against girls. And when girls get five dollars an hour for babysitting, they don't usually realize that they're being discriminated against."

Bégin urges girls who babysit to discuss this kind of discrimination with their employers. If that doesn't get them better pay, she recommends girls switch from babysitting to snow shoveling

At an Equal Pay Day demonstration in Ontario, women were asked to wear red because "the gender pay gap leaves women in the red."

or lawn mowing. Even so, it's the system that should be changing, not the girls.

You may remember from the introduction to this book that according to Statistics Canada, in 2015, Canadian females earned eighty-seven cents for every dollar earned by Canadian males.

That isn't great, but things used to be even worse.

In the 1960s American women made fifty-nine cents for every dollar earned by American men. In those days most middle- and upper-class women did not work outside the home. As Nadia Abushanab Higgins points out in her book *Feminism: Reinventing the F-Word*, during the 1960s working women were "mostly women of color and white working-class women." Abushanab Higgins reports that today, 40 percent of American mothers are the family breadwinners!

Even though the gender gap in earnings has fluctuated over time, white men still earn more money than anyone else. Equal Pay Day is an important day on the feminist calendar. Created in the United States in 1996 by the National Committee on Pay Equity, it marks how far into the year women must work to earn what men earned in the previous year. In 2018 Equal Pay Day was

marked in the United States on April 10. Equal Pay Day is marked in Canada too. In 2017 it took place on April 11.

Pay inequity even affects Hollywood stars. In a 2017 interview with *Marie Claire UK*, actor Natalie Portman revealed she is paid far less than her male co-stars. "We get paid a lot," she said, "so it's hard to complain, but the disparity is crazy…Compared to men, in most professions, women make 80 cents to the dollar. In Hollywood, we are making 30 cents to the dollar." Many other actors have since come forward to protest pay inequity in their industry. They include Jennifer Lawrence, Reese Witherspoon, Charlize Theron, Debra Messing and Eva Longoria.

When actor and comedian Amy Schumer learned that Chris Rock and Dave Chappelle had each earned $20 million for their comedy specials, she insisted on more money from Netflix for her comedy special *The Leather Special*. Even then, she still didn't get paid $20 million.

Oprah Winfrey is a veteran in the fight for pay equity. When she was doing *The Oprah Winfrey Show* she noticed that her female producers were being paid less than their male counter-parts. When she discussed this with her boss, he told her, "They're only girls."

To which Oprah replied: "Either they're gonna get raises, or I'm gonna sit down." By that Oprah meant if the situation was not rectified, she was prepared to quit her job!

Longtime *E! News* anchor Catt Sadler did just that. In December 2017 she quit her job after learning her co-host Jason Kennedy was earning a lot more money than she was.

Actress Sandra Bullock says pay inequity in Hollywood is part of a bigger problem—systemic discrimination. In 2015 she told *Variety*: "Watch, we're going to walk down the red carpet, I'm going to be asked about my dress and my hair while the man standing next to me will be asked about his performance and political issues."

In recent years the gender pay gap has become a controversial topic. Many people, including feminist researchers, attribute the gap to workplace sexism. But there are others who blame women, arguing that

*In 2017 E! News anchor Catt Sadler quit her job after learning that her male co-host was being paid far more than she was.*

women are making a lifestyle choice by taking jobs that are less well paying in order to focus on raising their families. In a 2014 article on *Breitbart*, a far-right (extremely conservative) American news and commentary website, Jason Scheurer called the gender pay gap "a lie" and suggested that if there really was a gender pay gap, "why wouldn't *every* employer only hire women to save money and increase profits? Where are all the female-only companies?"

I have an answer for Scheurer: It's true that some women are financially able to choose to work part time (or not at all) so they can raise their families. But in a truly equitable world, where fathers were equally responsible for childcare and household chores, women would have more options—including the option to focus more on their careers.

## MAKING EQUAL PAY A LEGAL RIGHT

In the United States the Equal Pay Act of 1963 prohibited discrimination on account of gender in the payment of wages. But even with that legislation, pay inequity has continued. In October 2017 the state of California became the eighth American jurisdiction to introduce a pay-equity measure, making it illegal for employers to ask job candidates about their previous salaries. This is because employers often base salaries on what their employees have earned at previous jobs. The pay-equity measure also prohibits employers from reporting their former employees' salaries. This new legislation is an important way to keep women from lagging behind on the pay scale.

Only two Canadian provinces, Quebec and Ontario, have proactive pay-equity legislation. Quebec's Pay Equity Act has been in place since 1996. It requires all businesses with ten or more employees to ensure that regardless of their gender, workers are paid the same for work of equal value. Unlike the equal-pay-for-equal-work approach, which requires that men and women must be doing the same job in order to ensure equal pay, Quebec's Pay Equity Act looks at classes of jobs done primarily by men in a specific organization and compares them with equivalent classes of jobs done primarily by women in the same organization. For example, Quebec's Pay Equity Act ensures that a hotel doorman is paid the same hourly wage as a chambermaid.

With so many men fighting overseas during World War II, women had to do jobs that had been seen as traditionally male. This female aircraft worker checks electrical assemblies in Burbank, CA.

## MALE-DOMINATED PROFESSIONS

Catharine Beecher did not believe women should have the right to vote. A nineteenth-century American educator (and sister of the famous *abolitionist* Harriet Beecher Stowe), Beecher believed a woman's place was in the home—or at the chalkboard.

"Most happily," Beecher wrote, "the education necessary to fit a woman to be a teacher is exactly the one that best fits her for that domestic relation she is primarily designed to fill."

I like to imagine Beecher's expression if she could see today's world, where women are employed in every sphere, from masonry to medicine to space exploration.

Teaching and nursing are examples of professions many of us still associate with women. According to the United States Department of Labor, in 1975 only 3 percent of registered nurses were men. That percentage rose to 5.5 percent in 1990 and to 9 percent in 2015. In 1975, 14.6 percent of American elementary schoolteachers were men. By 1990 that number had risen only to 14.8 percent. In 2012 (the latest year for which this statistic was available), 18.3 percent of elementary schoolteachers were male.

You might be surprised to learn that until the American Civil War, most nurses, teachers and librarians were men. As Christine L. Williams explains in *Still a Man's World*, "Men performed most of the nursing tasks during the Revolutionary War; George Washington ordered the employment of women as nurses only if adequate numbers of male surgeons' mates could not be found." Some 620,000 men died during the Civil War, leading to a shortage of men in the American labor force. And because women were paid considerably less than men, it made economic sense to hire them to work as nurses, teachers and librarians. By 1900 these professions had been redefined as "feminine" and "maternal."

In principle at least, today's girls and women can enter any field they choose. In reality, many professions remain male dominated. Researchers have focused in particular on the gender disparity in STEM, which stands for science, technology, engineering and mathematics. As Anne-Marie Slaughter points out, only 6 percent of the world's mechanical engineers are women.

British businesswoman Stephanie Shirley believes this situation has something to do with the stereotype of the male computer geek. In 1962 Shirley founded a software company that employed only female programmers. Shirley believes that children as young as two years old—and in particular girls—

*Ashley Speicher believes girls should learn to code. Speicher should know. She's the software engineering manager for Xbox.*

should be learning to code, which means using algorithms to solve problems.

However, most of today's coders are male. In 1984, 37 percent of American computer science majors were female. In 2014 that percentage had decreased to 18 percent. Too many girls continue to see STEM subjects as difficult and boring. Movies, TV and books do not provide many female-techie role models. The "boys' club" culture of the tech industry is also a problem. Some women leave the industry because they find the culture so toxic.

Ashley Speicher is the software engineering manager for Xbox. She thinks another reason girls avoid learning to code is they think it's not creative. That isn't true, says Speicher: "When you're working on a coding project, it's incredibly creative...Girls should code. It's an incredibly fun thing to do as your job."

Black Girls CODE was founded in 2011 by Kimberly Bryant, who says, "The Black Girls CODE mission [is] to introduce programming and technology to a new generation of coders, coders who will become builders of technological innovation and of their own futures." The organization is devoted to empowering young girls of color to become innovators in STEM fields, and showing the world that girls of every color have the skills to become the programmers of tomorrow. Their goal is to grow the number of women of color working in technology and provide African American youth with the skills to occupy some of the 1.4 million computing job openings expected to be available in the U.S. by 2020.

## STEM (AND SOMETIMES STEAM) IN THE SCHOOLS

Sophie, fourteen, a tenth-grader at The Study, an all-girls school in Montreal, thinks she might want to be an architect one day. "I visited Chicago and saw many famous, inspiring buildings. But none that I heard of were designed or built by women. I thought that was very unfortunate," says Sophie.

STEM has been part of the curriculum at Sophie's school for nearly twenty years. In 2011 the school decided to use the acronym STEAM instead of STEM to demonstrate its recognition that the arts (that's what the A stands for) are also an essential part of its students' education.

On the school's ground floor, next to the auditorium, is what is known as a MakerSpace. "It's a place to create, invent and dream. Some of the tools used in the MakerSpace are twenty-first-century equivalents of those once used in an old-fashioned shop class," explains Amalia Liogas, the school's IT director. Equipment here includes a laser cutter (the eighth-grade girls

## WHO SAYS GIRLS DON'T LIKE TO GET THEIR HANDS DIRTY?

In November 2016 Bernie Wolfe Community School in Winnipeg, Manitoba, hosted an event called Unlocking the Tool Box. Sixty-eight fifth-grade girls got to meet women who work in trades and professions that tend to be male dominated. The girls also got their hands dirty by trying out some of the skills these women use on the job.

"Women are underrepresented in trades and STEM. We want to show students that the artistry, skill and passion for the work you do is not limited by your gender," said Catherine Westlake, a career-development teacher with the River East Transcona School Division and one of the organizers of the event.

The day's experts included a plumber, a carpenter, a mason and an electrician, as well as women in STEM professions. The fifth-grade girls laid brick, wired a circuit and assembled and sanded a picture frame.

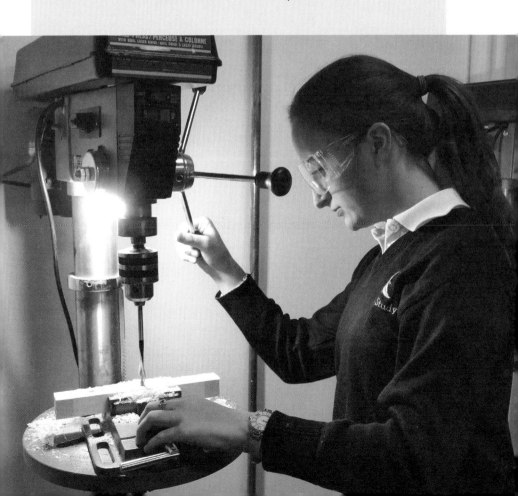

Girls in FIRST® (or FLL, FIRST® Lego League) build cool LEGO robots and take part in challenges and competitions.

will use it later in the year to cut wood and steel for the lamps they will be building); a CNC mill, which uses drill bits to cut; and thousands of LEGO pieces that students, including those in the school's robotics club, use to build robots.

In 2013 the school began teaching coding to its kindergarten students. On the day I visited the MakerSpace, teacher Lisa Jacobsen was working with a third-grade class. "The students are learning how, unlike people, a computer or robot can't guess what you're thinking," Ms. Jacobsen explained. To teach her class that programmers must give precise instructions in a language the computer or robot understands, she divided her class into pairs—one girl was the robot; the other, the programmer. April was programming her friend Samantha. "I tell her 'Go right' or 'Go left,' 'Go forward,' 'Stop' and she does it," April explained.

Learning how to overcome obstacles was part of the afternoon's lesson. "It can be frustrating when the robot doesn't do what you want it to, but you have to get creative and find another way. It takes persistence and many iterations to get a computer or robot to do exactly what you want it to," said Ms. Jacobsen.

Another student in the class, Olivia, said that when she is grown up, she'd like to make drones. "I have drones at my house, but they don't work well. I'd improve them. I'd use my drone for walking the dog," she said.

When Lela was in the second grade, she and a group of classmates made a caterpillar robot. "The caterpillar moved its head up and down. We controlled our animals with an iPad," she explained.

Isabella, fourteen, had always loved math. "But my love for technology and physics has grown here," she explained. Isabella was considering a career in astrophysics. "It sounds cool. I consider myself a geek and a nerd. In movies the stereotypical geeks are guys. There aren't very many girl geeks in Hollywood."

# THE GLASS CEILING

The term *glass ceiling* is a metaphor used to describe the invisible barrier that prevents women—and members of minority groups— from rising to the highest ranks in the workplace. The term was popularized in 1986 by an article written by Carol Hymowitz and Timothy D. Schellhardt for the *Wall Street Journal*.

Concordia University management professor Steven
Appelbaum and a team of researchers have found that "only three
percent of top executives among Fortune 500 firms are women."
Appelbaum predicts that at the rate we are going, we will not
reach gender equality in the boardroom until 2081! He believes
societal attitudes are largely to blame. "Women," says Appelbaum,
"are still perceived as inferior leaders despite the fact that they
often possess the qualities that make excellent senior managers."

Another issue is that women who work outside the home
experience more conflict between their work and family obliga-
tions than men do. "Companies tend to favor those who can get
there early, stay late, answer emails at all hours and travel when-
ever necessary. For many mothers of young children that's just
impossible," says Appelbaum.

Like Appelbaum, some researchers suggest that women's
presence in the highest-level positions violates societal norms and
threatens men. Faced with the glass ceiling, some women decide
to leave corporations and go into business for themselves.

Here's something else to consider: many individuals in high-
level positions credit a mentor for contributing to their career
success. Fewer women in the highest ranks in the workplace
means fewer female mentors. Male mentors may prefer to mentor
other men.

How will today's girls be able to shatter the glass ceiling?
Education is one answer. Women with university degrees, especially master's degrees in business, are more likely to be hired
for high management positions. Corporations and organizations must make changes too. They need to not only hire but also
promote women and minorities. They also need to create workplaces that are more family friendly by providing services such as
on-site daycare.

## NOT JUST A BACKUP SINGER!
# *Emily Skahan is a feminist!*

Singer-songwriter Emily Skahan is part of Motel Raphaël, a popular Montreal-based band. Skahan, 28, and her band have performed at the Osheaga Music and Arts Festival, the Montreal Jazz Festival and the South by Southwest Conference and Festivals in Austin, Texas. The band's best-known song is "Ghosts." At the time I interviewed Skahan, the band was working on its third album.

"Like many industries, music is male dominated," says Skahan. " People often expect women in music to be backup singers. When we arrive at a venue, I've noticed that the sound men look to the male musicians in our band—we have a male drummer and a male bassist— if they have questions about setup."

Skahan, who got into music seriously when she was in tenth grade, has always been a feminist. "It's important for young girls to identify as feminists in a world that sees feminism in a negative way. It's important to pull yourself away from people who make you doubt yourself when you demand equal rights. You're not asking for a unicorn. Feminism is not impossible. It's tangible. We can do it together."

Here's a related term you've probably never heard of: the *sticky floor*. Sociologist Catherine White Berheide came up with it in the 1990s to refer to the phenomenon of women being trapped in low-paying jobs without much hope of advancement. Many of the women caught on the sticky floor work in what are known as pink-collar jobs—for example, waitressing and office work. Generally, these kinds of jobs pay poorly, hours can be long, and there is little or no opportunity for promotion. These women are far less privileged than those who are bumping up against the glass ceiling.

There are systemic barriers to women's success in the workplace whether they are doing pink-collar work or working as

executives. In 2011 Sindhuja Rajamaran, who was fourteen at the time, was awarded the Guinness World Record for being the world's youngest CEO. Rajamaran, who is from Chennai, India, is the CEO of Seppan Entertainment, an animation company. Rajamaran had several mentors, including her dad, who is also in the animation business.

Not all girls have access to a mentor. Lindsay Hyde has been working to change that. In 2000, Hyde, who was then a freshman at Harvard University, founded a nonprofit organization called Strong Women, Strong Girls. SWSG works with schools and community centers in Boston and Pittsburgh. Through SWSG, girls are mentored by college women, who in turn are mentored by professional women. As we have seen, few professional women in today's workplace had female role

*At the age of 14, Sindhuja Rajamaran was India's youngest CEO.*

models to inspire them. Programs like SWSG give these women an opportunity to provide the kind of career support they wish they had had.

## STANDING TALL IN EVERY WAY
# Denise Donlon is a feminist!

"There is definitely a glass ceiling. Sometimes it feels like a cement ceiling. I may have shattered it, but I have shards of glass stuck in my forehead," Denise Donlon told me during a phone interview. Donlon, 61, was Sony Music Canada's first female president. She was also executive director of CBC Radio's English-language services.

I met Donlon in the spring of 2017, when she was in Montreal to promote her memoir, *Fearless as Possible (Under the Circumstances)*. Donlon urges young women not to fear the word *feminist*. "It's a word that must be owned. All it means at the end of the day is equality. It's too soft to call yourself a humanist."

Donlon is six feet tall. In her memoir she recounts how she used to slouch in high school. Her advice for tall girls applies to girls and women of every height: "Stand up straight. It's not only physical; it's a metaphor for how you carry yourself in the world...Even if you don't feel strong and worthy, you can only be yourself. Taking the step forward—even if you fail—is 100 times better than standing in one place," she says.

During her presentation in Montreal, Donlon showed the audience an image of a lipsticked red mouth caressing a white snake. The image was used to promote *Slide It In*, the sixth album of a band named Whitesnake. In 1984 someone handed Donlon a backstage pass with that image on it. She balked (in those days the image was considered quite scandalous) but ended up taking the pass (she tried to hide it in her pocket).

Donlon and I discussed how the world has changed since 1984. Hopefully that misogynistic image and slogan would be unacceptable today. Yet it is still not always easy to stand up for ourselves. Here's Donlon's advice: "When you're young, you're trying so desperately hard to be liked and to succeed. Young women need to be very mindful of misogyny. You have to say, 'That is unfair to women.'"

# SEXUAL HARASSMENT IN THE WORKPLACE

*Sexual harassment* refers to behavior of a sexual nature that a person finds offensive or unwelcome. Sexual harassment can include any unwanted sexual attention—verbal or physical—as well as *sexual coercion*, which refers to gaining sexual cooperation in exchange for job-related outcomes such as a raise or a part in a movie.

Sexual harassment is a widespread problem in the workplace, affecting both women and men. According to a 2014 study by the Angus Reid Institute, 28 percent of Canadians have experienced sexual harassment in their place of work or at a work-related function. Women, however, were more than three times as likely as men to experience sexual harassment. An American study released in 2015 suggested that one in three American women has been sexually harassed in her workplace.

Not all employees report sexual harassment to their employers. According to the Angus Reid study, one-quarter of the employees who *did* report sexual harassment or unwanted sexual contact found their employers to be "unresponsive and dismissive."

In Canada, members of the military, Parliament, the Royal Canadian Mounted Police (RCMP) and the Canadian Broadcasting Corporation (CBC) have been accused of sexual harassment or misconduct and assault. In 2014 Justin Trudeau, at that time leader of the Liberal Party, expelled two members of Parliament, Scott Andrews and Massimo Pacetti, from the party after seeing an independent report on allegations of their inappropriate behavior with two female members of Parliament.

A class-action lawsuit against the RCMP is the first gender-harassment class-action lawsuit in Canadian history. The lawsuit alleges sexual harassment and discrimination in Canada's

Members of the Royal Canadian Mounted Police (RCMP), Canada's federal and national police force, have been accused of sexual harassment, misconduct and assault.

national police force. The #MeToo movement inspired many past and present female RCMP members to come forward to talk about their experiences and join the lawsuit. The claims were supposed to have been filed by February 2018, but because of the huge number of claimants, lawyers requested an extension. Toronto-based lawyer Megan McPhee, who is working on the case, said she "wouldn't be surprised" if there were as many as 4,000 claimants by the time the process is completed.

Many other institutions are looking at improved ways of dealing with sexual harassment in the workplace. But eliminating sexual harassment will not be easy. It does not help that there are people in high positions who fail to see sexual harassment as a serious problem in the workplace. In 2015 Tom Lawson, Canada's Chief of the Defence Staff at the time, infuriated many Canadians when he said in a CBC interview that sexual harassment existed "because we're biologically wired in a certain way and there will be those who believe it is a reasonable thing to press themselves and their desires on others."

We all knew that sexual harassment in the workplace existed. But it was really just in October 2017, when the online community got involved, that the world finally understood the pervasiveness of sexual harassment. That was when, following allegations of sexual misconduct against Hollywood film producer Harvey Weinstein, the #MeToo hashtag was first used.

Civil rights activist Tarana Burke is the founder of the #MeToo movement.

The phrase *Me Too* was coined by social activist Tarana Burke in 2007. Ten years later, shortly after the allegations against Weinstein were made public, actor Alyssa Milano popularized the phrase on Twitter by writing: "If all the women who have been sexually harassed or assaulted wrote 'Me too' as a status, we might give people a sense of the magnitude of the problem."

In the first twenty-four hours after it appeared on social media, #MeToo was used by more than 4 million people in over 12 million posts. The hashtag broke the silence surrounding sexual harassment and assault. In the weeks that followed, many other well-known, powerful men—actors, directors, producers, celebrity chefs…the list goes on and on—were accused of sexual harassment and assault.

Of course the allegations that made the news involved famous men. What about all the other male bosses out there? You don't have to be rich or famous to wield your power inappropriately. "There have been stunning accounts of farmworkers harassed in the field, factory workers on lines, restaurant workers," said feminist scholar and University of Michigan law professor Catharine MacKinnon.

When female celebrities speak out and share their stories, women who are less well known and less powerful are inspired

Many women on the red carpet wore black at the 75th Golden Globe Awards ceremony as a way of protesting sexual harassment and assault in the workplace.

to add their voices to the conversation. That is exactly what happened in November 2017 when the Alianza Nacional de Campesinas (National Farmworkers Women's Alliance), an organization representing some 700,000 female American farmworkers, published a letter in *Time* magazine about how common it is for these women to be harassed and assaulted on the job.

That letter in turn inspired another movement known as Time's Up. This movement, which aims to provide legal support to women who cannot otherwise afford it, was founded on the first day of 2018. More than 300 American and British women, many from the entertainment industry, signed an announcement published in the *New York Times*. They have raised over $13 million for a legal defense fund that will help those who lack access to the media, and who cannot afford to pay a lawyer, to speak up about sexual harassment and assault in the workplace. The women behind the Time's Up movement also called for women on the red carpet at the 75th Golden Globe Awards to wear black to the awards ceremony and to speak out against

## CALLING OUT SEXUAL HARASSMENT LIVE ON AIR

Since 2015 there has been a disturbing trend in Canadian live television. Female reporters doing live TV broadcasts have been sexually harassed on air by men screaming obscene phrases at them. But these women are fighting back! In August 2017 at Montreal's Osheaga Music and Arts Festival, a man approached Radio-Canada reporter Valerie-Micaela Bain and kissed her. Bain pushed him aside and continued her report. Later, in a Facebook post, Bain wrote: *You wouldn't kiss me if you saw me on the street, it's not suddenly acceptable because I'm a woman in front of a live camera on TV…kissing someone without consent is a no.* A few days later, Bain informed her Facebook followers that the man had apologized. Bain hopes others will learn from her experience: "I hope that this incident will remind us that we must not trivialize the attacks, no matter how small," she said.

sexual harassment and assault in the workplace. It is not an exaggeration to say that on January 7, the night of the Golden Globes, the Time's Up movement stole the show.

Not everyone supports the #MeToo and Time's Up movements. Many saw the October 2018 appointment of Brett Kavanaugh to the US Supreme Court as proof of backlash against women's progress. Christine Blasey Ford, a Stanford University psychology professor, testified that he had attempted to rape her while they were in high school. Kavanaugh was still appointed. The controversy sparked discussion in homes, schools, offices and online about consent, sexual violence and the challenges associated with sharing details of a traumatic experience.

Feeling comfortable and safe in our workplaces is another basic human right. #MeToo and Time's Up are powerful and important ways for women (and their allies) to say they have had enough, that they will no longer accept sexual harassment and that they will stand up not only for themselves, but also for those who find it difficult to speak up. By refusing to stay silent about sexual harassment and assault on the job, by standing up for ourselves and each other, we can feel more secure in our workplaces—and concentrate on the work we have been hired to do.

*Chapter Six*

# INTERSECTIONALITY: DIVERSE AND INCLUSIVE FEMINISM

**R**emember bell hooks from chapter 1 and how she realized she was the only black woman in her feminism classes? hooks is often credited for being one of the first feminists to recognize racist biases in feminist thinking—and to call for change.

The theory of intersectionality goes even further. The term was popularized in 1989 by American feminist legal scholar and activist Kimberlé Williams Crenshaw, and it refers to how people's experiences of oppression are shaped by their race, class, gender, ethnicity and sexuality. All these (and other) aspects of our identity intersect, like in those Venn diagrams you learned about in math class.

In a paper Crenshaw published in the *University of Chicago Legal Forum*, she examined how the intersection of race and gender shapes the way black men and women experience the legal system. She demonstrated that black women's claims were taken less seriously than those of black men. Crenshaw drew attention to what she called "the double bind of race and gender."

Have you heard the expression "Check your privilege"? It is often used to remind us that the body and life we are born with come with certain privileges. It also reminds us to be aware of the experience of those with fewer privileges.

Here's an example to help you understand privilege and intersectionality. Imagine a wealthy, healthy, white, heterosexual man trying to access decent health care for his child. Probably not too difficult. He can get time off from work; he probably has access to a car; his word is trusted…Now imagine that experience from the point of view of a poor, disabled, nonwhite, gay or trans woman.

Here's another example. Psychology professor Michael Climan asked his male students to consider what it would feel like to be a woman walking alone at night who suddenly becomes aware of a man walking close behind her. Climan suggested to his male students that when they find themselves in this situation they take a simple action: cross to the other side of the street. Though Climan did not ask his students to check their privilege, that was essentially his message. He was encouraging the young men in his class to imagine being someone else—the woman walking ahead of them on the sidewalk—and to find a way to ease her discomfort.

But the person who most eloquently explained to me the importance of an intersectional approach to feminism was Anita Reddy, an English teacher at Montreal's Royal West Academy, who helps supervise the school's feminism club—a group of about twenty students who meet every Friday at lunch to discuss issues having to do with feminism and who raise money to support a local women's shelter.

This is what Reddy told me: "I think intersectionality is the only viable future for feminism. Feminism is about all of our identities as women. If we don't acknowledge the differences between us, how can we say we stand for the same thing? We have to

The future of feminism depends on intersectionality. All women's voices need to be heard, not only the voices of those who are most privileged.

acknowledge that we don't all have the same strength of voice in the movement."

In previous chapters I have referred to the particular challenges faced by women of color. In this chapter we will look more deeply into their experience as well as the experience of Indigenous, LGBTQ+ and disabled women, and women who are sex workers.

Privilege means power. Here's something I tell my students: "You are teenagers now, whose parents and teachers have power over you. But one day not too long from now, when you have completed your studies and established careers and families, you will be the ones with power. How you wield your power, and how you treat those who are less privileged than you are, is perhaps the best indication of who you really are."

American scholar Patricia Hill Collins wrote about how black women are doubly discriminated against.

## RACE

In her 1990 book *Black Feminist Thought: Knowledge, Consciousness, and the Politics of Empowerment*, Patricia Hill Collins describes how African American women face the double burden of racial and gender discrimination. Hill Collins explores the work of black feminists and writers, including bell hooks and Alice Walker (whose novel *The Color Purple* won the 1983 Pulitzer Prize for Fiction).

In her book *Feminism is for Everybody: Passionate Politics*, bell hooks writes: "All white women in this country [the United States] know that whiteness is a privileged category."

As you learned in chapter 5, black women and other women of color were part of the labor force well before their white sisters. Furthermore, women of color have a history of working at arduous, low-paying jobs. According to the Economic Policy

Institute, black women work longer hours than Caucasian women and earn less than them in every type of job, whether it is working as a store clerk or as a surgeon.

Black women experience poverty at a higher rate than any other group, too, with the exception of Indigenous women. This means black and Indigenous women have less income and wealth than other members of society. According to the Institute for Women's Policy Research, in 2014 black women had the highest unemployment rate (10.5 percent) among women, compared to 5.2 percent for white women.

## DON'T LEAVE HOME WITHOUT YOUR SUPER CAPE!

In 2017 Lena Waithe became the first black woman to win a Primetime Emmy Award for Outstanding Writing for a Comedy Series. Waithe, who plays Denise in the Netflix series *Master of None*, won the Emmy for her script "Thanksgiving." The episode spans 22 years, following Denise as she reveals to her family that she is gay. The prize-winning script is based on Waithe's own experience of coming out to her family.

In her acceptance speech, Waithe gave a shout-out to her "LGBTQIA family" (the extra letters stand for *intersex* and *asexual*). She told the LGBTQIA community, "I see each and every one of you. The things that make us different…these are our superpowers. Every day when you walk out the door and put on your imaginary cape, go out there and conquer the world, because the world would not be as beautiful without us in it."

The situation is especially dire for black women in low-income jobs. In 2015 Deborah Sweeney, a driver for the Newark Public Schools, told NBC News that she had been the victim of verbal, physical and sexual abuse in her workplace. Because she was the principal breadwinner for her family, Sweeney was unable to quit her job. As she pointed out, "If it would have been a white woman, all hell would have broke through."

## INDIGENEITY

"Indigenous women face multiple challenges—whether they live on reserve or in cities," said Nakuset, executive director of Montreal's Native Women's Shelter, the only shelter in the city that provides services exclusively to Indigenous women and their children.

"On reserve, depending on the community, those challenges can include no running water, no school, inadequate housing, lack of social services and jobs. There's also unbelievable racism from anyone working in a government building. When Indigenous girls and women come to the city, they think they'll find something better. Instead, they often face a new kind of racism. People don't want to rent to you. They assume you have drug or alcohol problems. Youth protection is much quicker to take your children away," said Nakuset.

Many of Canada's Indigenous women live in poverty and lack the opportunity to complete high school and continue on to college and university. Canada's Indigenous women report a far greater incidence of physical and sexual abuse than non-Indigenous women. These problems have been linked in part to the Canadian government's residential school system (1831–1996), which forcibly removed some 150,000 Indigenous children from their families and sent them to residential school, where they were separated from their own culture and language. Over 3,000 of these children died at the schools or when they ran away, trying to return home. In 2009 Canada established the Truth and Reconciliation Commission, whose task it was to "acknowledge the past through truth-telling." They gathered testimony from men and women across the country. It soon became clear that the effects of the residential school system extend through many generations. The commission's work ended in 2015 when it presented 94 Calls to Action to "redress the legacy of residential schools and advance the process of Canadian reconciliation."

Nakuset, executive director of Montreal's Native Women's Shelter, says Indigenous women face systemic discrimination. She works to support Indigenous women who have moved to the city.

There are many ways we can perform acts of reconciliation. We can learn more about the history of residential schools, attend Indigenous cultural events such as powwows and read books by Indigenous authors. We can research whose traditional lands we live and go to school on. I live and work in Montreal, the traditional lands of the KanienÐkehá:ka Nation. We can raise money for awards such as Canada's Emerging Indigenous Voices award, which supports the work of new Indigenous authors.

At Eastview Public School in Scarborough, Ontario, students begin the day not only by singing the national anthem, but also by performing a smudging ceremony in which medicinal plants are burned to create smoke—a traditional Indigenous ritual that aims to purify a soul or place. Morning announcements at the school acknowledge that the campus is located on First Nations and Métis territories. One-third of Eastview's students identify as First Nations, Inuit or Métis. "Before I came to this school, I had no idea about the First Nations," said Maria, an eighth-grader at the school.

In Canada, Indigenous women account for 3 percent of the female population. Yet 10 percent of all females murdered in Canada are Indigenous. There is much discussion about the number of Indigenous Canadian women who have gone missing or been murdered in the last thirty years. Estimates range between 500 and 1,100. The Native Women's Association of Canada has information on 582 cases.

The name Highway of Tears was given to a roughly 700-kilometer stretch of highway between Prince George and Prince Rupert, British Columbia. That is because so many Indigenous women have disappeared or been found murdered along this route, which has been popular with hitchhikers. Poverty plays a role here too. The women who hitchhike along this stretch of road tend to be poor and cannot afford other ways to travel. For them, the highway holds promise of a new job in the city.

According to the *Globe and Mail* newspaper, Indigenous women in Canada are roughly seven times more likely than non-Indigenous women to be murdered by serial killers. Sherry Lewis, executive director of the Native Women's Association of Canada, is not alone in believing that the rest of the country has turned a blind eye to the plight of Indigenous women. "One non-aboriginal woman goes missing and all of a sudden there was a media frenzy," Lewis has said.

In September 2016 the Canadian government finally took action by launching the National Inquiry into Missing and Murdered Indigenous Women and Girls. The MMIWG commissioners collect testimonies from the families of missing and

The REDress Project is on permanent exhibit at Winnipeg's Canadian Museum of Human Rights. Started in 2010 by Métis artist Jaime Black, the project serves as a reminder of the many missing and murdered Indigenous women and girls in Canada.

murdered Indigenous women and girls. They ask family members to send photographs and share stories about their loved ones. They are also looking at the systemic causes of all forms of violence against Indigenous girls and women and investigating how police, social workers and other officials have handled these cases.

In the United States, Indigenous women are also far more likely to be victims of violence than non-Indigenous women are. According to the Indian Law Resource Center, a majority of American Indian and Alaskan Native women have experienced violence. The organization's Safe Women, Strong Nations project works to help restore safety to Indigenous women.

As in Canada, the American Indigenous community is also dealing with the legacy of residential schools. In the United States, as far back as the late 1800s, Christian missionaries established

A participant in the Greater Than Fear Rally and March in Rochester, MN, in October 2018. The rally and march were held in response to President Trump's rally in downtown Rochester.

what were known as Native American boarding schools. Here, too, many students were intimidated and abused. And because one of the goals of these schools was *assimilation* (the process by which a person's culture becomes absorbed into the dominant culture), many of the students lost their own language and culture.

The Safe Women, Strong Nations project works in partnership with Native women's organizations and American Indian and Alaskan Native nations to end violence and provide legal advice. In Canada, the Native Women's Association does similar work. Its Sisters in Spirit project focused on research, education and policy relating to violence against Indigenous women.

The Sisters in Spirit web page began with a prayer called "Grandmother Moon." It included the moving line *Creator, keep our sisters safe from harm.* Unfortunately the government cut funding to the Sisters in Spirit project in 2010.

Indigenous peoples are an important part of our multicultural society and our history. The original inhabitants of Canada and the United States are the keepers of culture, language and values. Though Indigenous women have faced and continue to face tremendous challenges, they play important leadership roles in their communities and are often the strongest advocates for change. These women's remarkable strength and resilience serve as inspiration to all of us.

## WISE ADVICE FROM A JEWISH INDIAN
### *Nakuset is a feminist!*

"I'm a Jewish Indian," said Nakuset, executive director of Montreal's Native Women's Shelter. Born to a Cree family in Manitoba, Nakuset was adopted and raised by a Jewish family in Montreal. The name Nakuset is a spirit name given to her by an Indigenous elder. It means "sun."

What advice does Nakuset have for Indigenous and non-Indigenous young people? "Learn about Indigenous history. It's not in the history books. Read the 94 Calls to Action from the Truth and Reconciliation Commission of Canada report. Learn about residential schools, and missing and murdered Indigenous women. When you see a homeless woman on the street, offer her food, say hello, ask where she is from. Be kind—as we were once kind to you," she said.

## FACELESS DOLLS TELL A STORY ABOUT MMIWG

In March 2012 the Native Women's Association of Canada (NWAC) launched the Faceless Dolls Project. It is a traveling art exhibit created in memory of the more than 600 missing and murdered Indigenous girls and women. It continues to be exhibited at schools and community centers across the country. The original 600 dolls were made from felt and hand cut by Cree artist Gloria Larocque. The NWAC was familiar with Larocque's work because of her 2007 Aboriginal Angel Doll Project. "I did that project to highlight the beauty and resilience of Indigenous womanhood," Larocque told me.

Larocque lives on Treaty 8 territory in Alberta. As a child she was in and out of foster care. "I learned to sew quite young in a foster home. Sewing took me away from my troubles and let me turn them into something beautiful," she said. As an adult, Larocque did volunteer work in Vancouver's Downtown Eastside, where she met many Indigenous women. "I realized that just by being born I was part of the problem. I wondered, How can I raise my own voice?" she said.

Art was her answer. No two of Larocque's dolls are the same—a way of reminding those who view the exhibit that Indigenous women are made faceless by society, and that every single missing and murdered Indigenous girl and woman was a unique and valued individual. "Feminism hasn't worked for Indigenous women. We've been completely left out. Indigenous women need to have their own wave of feminism. Although I agree with that very much, I have also learned how much Indigenous women have exerted our own strength and resiliency over the years," said Larocque.

Sadly, in 2016 nearly 500 dolls decorated by families of missing and murdered Indigenous women disappeared after they were displayed in Winnipeg. Those dolls have still not been recovered.

# GENDER AND SEXUALITY

LGBTQ+ girls and women face discrimination in every area of their lives. They are harassed and sometimes attacked on the streets, and they are discriminated against in the workplace.

Trans individuals—those who present, live or identify as a gender other than the one they were born with—are especially vulnerable to violence. That vulnerability increases for trans women and even more so for trans women of color.

Not surprisingly, LGBTQ+ youth who do not get adequate support from their families and communities may turn to alcohol and drugs—and even suicide. The risk of substance abuse and suicide is estimated to be fourteen times higher for LGBTQ+ youth than for their straight peers.

Once again, money helps tell the story. According to the University of California Los Angeles's Williams Institute, members of the LGBTQ+ community are more likely to be poor than cisgender individuals. The Williams Institute has found that lesbian and bisexual women are especially vulnerable to poverty. Twenty-four percent of American lesbian and bisexual women are poor, compared to 19 percent of heterosexual women. The poverty rate for American gay and heterosexual men is roughly equal at 13 percent. Lesbian and bisexual women frequently face discrimination in the workplace, earning lower salaries and having less opportunity for advancement. They are even more likely to be poor if they are non-white and/or raising young children and/or old.

In Canada, too, gay and bisexual men and women have had to contend with workplace discrimination. According to class-action suits filed in Ontario and Quebec against the government of Canada, some 40,000 individuals lost their

Like other marginalized groups, members of the LGBTQ+ community are at an increased risk of discrimination.

government jobs between the 1950s and 1990s because of their sexual orientation.

The Williams Institute has found that workplace discrimination against members of the LGBTQ+ community is prevalent across the United States. Researchers point to a 2014 survey in Mississippi, which found that 24 percent of LGBTQ+ respondents reported having experienced workplace discrimination. To make matters worse, in July 2017 the Trump administration's Department of Justice argued that an existing law, Title VII of the

Civil Rights Act of 1964, does not bar an employer from firing an employee because he or she is gay.

Thankfully, the news is not all bad. Many schools and workplaces are implementing strategies to support the LGBTQ+ community. One example is gender-neutral bathrooms, which have become standard at many schools.

Kristopher Wells, an assistant professor at the University of Alberta and co-director of its Institute for Sexual Minority Studies and Services, co-authored a guidebook to help educators support transgender youth. One of Wells's recommendations is that schools provide a non-gendered, single-stall washroom for use by any student wishing to use it.

Part of Wells's work involves running programs across the country for people aged five to ninety-five. He is also one of the founders of Camp fYrefly, a four-day leadership retreat for lesbian, gay, bisexual, trans-identified, two-spirited, intersexed, queer,

Founded in 2004, Camp fYrefly brings together LGBTQ+ youth for a four-day leadership retreat. Activities are designed to help young people explore their identity, build resilience and increase self-esteem.

## CHOOSING LIFE OVER DEATH

*Kristopher Wells is a feminist!*

"*Feminism* is not a dirty word. We want to support strong, vibrant girls and advocate for the world they want to create," said Kristopher Wells, co-director of the University of Alberta's Institute for Sexual Minority Studies and Services.

When I interviewed Wells, I asked what prompted him to do the work he does. His answer was so moving that I knew I had to share it with you.

"It was 1996. I was a new teacher in Alberta. At the time there were no human-rights protections on the grounds of sexual orientation. Gay teachers could be fired, and there were no safe spaces for LGBTQ youth. I was at a gay bar in Edmonton with my partner when I saw one of my students. I knew I couldn't acknowledge him.

"A few months later that same student committed suicide. That incident changed my life. I left teaching. I knew I wouldn't survive in the system as a closeted teacher. I had been that same kid at a different point in my life. But I made a different decision—I chose to live rather than to die. I joined a gay and lesbian youth group. When I told them I was a teacher, they said, *Do something.* So I did."

questioning and allied youth. When I interviewed Wells, I asked him what advice he has for LGBTQ+ youth. Here's what he said: "Be you. Be the very best you you can be. Take pride in your identity. You don't need to change. Society needs to change."

Canada is known for its support of LGBTQ+ rights. In 2005 Canada became the fourth country in the world to legalize same-sex marriage. In every Canadian province it is possible for transgender individuals to change their legal gender.

In November 2017 Prime Minister Justin Trudeau issued an apology to LGBTQ+ Canadians. He apologized for decades of what he described as "state-sponsored, systematic oppression and rejection." He called on Canadians to end discrimination against LGBTQ+ individuals who continue to face higher rates of aggression, violence, mental-health issues and homelessness.

The United States has lagged behind Canada in supporting members of the LBTQ+ community. It was not until 2015 that the United States Supreme Court ruled that same-sex marriage was legal in all jurisdictions. And some states do not allow transgender individuals to change their legal gender. Many states require proof of sex-reassignment surgery, something that is not necessary for Canadians wishing to change their legal gender.

## DISABILITY

The International Network of Women with Disabilities estimates that half a billion women worldwide are disabled. According to DAWN (DisAbled Women's Network) Canada, a cross-disability feminist organization founded in 1985 to support Canadian women with disabilities, one in five Canadian women lives with a disability.

Disabled girls and women are at a far higher risk of emotional, physical and sexual abuse than able-bodied women are. They risk being mistreated or abused by strangers, family members, personal attendants and health care professionals. DAWN's fact sheet reveals that 60 percent of

*Sarah Jama is an activist with DAWN Canada. She also runs the Disability Justice Network of Ontario, which is entirely youth led and run by women of color who have disabilities.*

women with disabilities have experienced some form of violence, and that women with disabilities are four times more likely to have been sexually assaulted than women without disabilities.

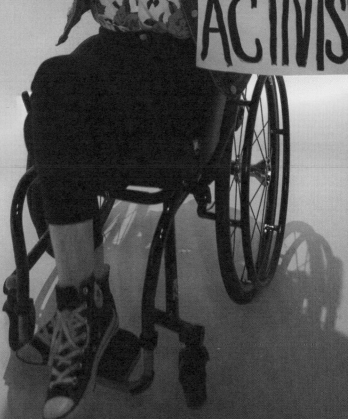
Eleanor Wheeler (aka Ellie Wheels) is a teen activist for people with disabilities.

Money is a problem for this group too. According to DAWN, the unemployment rate for disabled women is 75 percent. Fifty-eight percent of disabled women live on less than $10,000 per year. And of those women, 23 percent live on less than $5,000 per year.

Disabled individuals often report feeling ignored by the able-bodied community. That may be because for those of us who are able-bodied, seeing someone who is disabled is a reminder of our own vulnerability.

Just leaving the house can be more difficult for those who are disabled. Of the seventy-three metro stations in Montreal, only twelve have elevators to make them wheelchair accessible. This means that wheelchair-bound Montrealers have limited use of the city's subway system. The situation is only moderately better in many other major cities. Only one-quarter of the 270 underground stations in London, England, have step-free access (elevators, ramps and level surfaces) allowing individuals in wheelchairs to use them. Of New York City's 472 subway stations, only 19 percent are fully accessible to people in wheelchairs. Though New York City has been working to increase the number of wheelchair-accessible subway stations, activists estimate that it will take until 2100 before there is 100 percent accessibility.

The Internet is of particular value to those for whom mobility is a challenge. The International Network of Women with Disabilities, an organization with a strong online presence, makes it possible for disabled girls and women around the world to come together to share information and support each other. The INWWD website provides useful information and updates on relevant subjects—such as sexuality and disability—and tips for living independently.

## A LESSON IN BRAVERY
# Margot Vignal is a feminist!

I first met Margot Vignal in 2015 when I worked with her class at Westmount High School on a project called "Quebec Roots: The Place Where I Live." Margot, who is now 19, has cerebral palsy and has always needed a wheelchair to get around. For the Quebec Roots project, students from across Quebec tell their stories using words and photographs. Here's an excerpt from what Margot wrote: "When you're in a wheelchair, it feels as if people ignore and don't see you."

When Margot was a baby, a neuropediatrician (a children's doctor who specializes in neurological conditions) told her parents she would never be able to talk, walk, eat or even remember anything. "But now I can do all those things," said Margot when I visited her at the apartment she shares with her mom in Montreal.

Margot is a fighter. For many years she attended Mackay Centre School, a school for disabled students. But in 2014 she decided she needed the intellectual challenge of a regular high school. She met with the principals from Mackay Centre and Westmount High School, as well as several members of the school board—and convinced them to let her attend Westmount High. "This is who I am. This is what I want. And I need your help," she told them.

At around the same time that Margot was admitted to Westmount High, she came out to family and friends as bisexual. "Since I came out, I'm more myself, and I'm not hiding. When I was in the closet, I was not me. It takes time to find out who you are meant to be. Find people who will stick by your side and not be too judge-y," she said.

Margot plans to become a professional writer. She also enjoys working out. She trains once a week at Concordia University's PERFORM Centre Gym, and she has recently taken up boxing.

"I won my battle," she told me. Margot has good advice for other kids trying to overcome an obstacle: "Be brave."

Sociology professor Cecelia Benoit has spent years researching sex work. She believes we need to fight the stigma attached to sex work and the people who do it.

## SEX WORK

Cecilia Benoit remembers when her daughter, who was eleven years old at the time, came home from the playground in Victoria, British Columbia, and asked her parents what the word *whore* meant. "We explained how the word was very hurtful," said Benoit.

In 2016 Benoit won a Governor General's Award in recognition of her "contribution to the goal of equality for women and girls in Canada." A sociology professor at the University of Victoria, Benoit has done extensive research about sex work. She believes we must fight the stigma attached to sex work and the people who do it. "We have to think about what they're doing as an economic activity. This is the best people are able to do finding work considering their skill levels and life situations," she said during a phone interview.

It is too easy, said Benoit, to judge and stereotype sex workers. "People who sell sexual services are real people. They have real lives. They don't fit the stereotype of the whore. They could be your mother, your sister," she said.

According to a 2014 study from the University of Victoria's Institute of Gender and Health, 77 percent of Canadian sex workers are women. The study also found that 29 percent of sex workers had spent some of their childhood in foster care or another kind of government care.

In addition to dealing with the social stigma, sex workers often live in fear and isolation. Prostitution has been legal in Canada since 2013. However, in 2014 Canada's Conservative government passed the Protection of Communities and Exploited Persons Act (PCEPA), making it a criminal offense to purchase sexual services, communicate for that purpose and receive material benefit from sex work. Though the bill was designed to target *Johns* (male clients who purchase sexual services) and *pimps* (men who control prostitutes and arrange clients for them, taking part of their earnings in return), many sex workers, as well as those who advocate for their rights, believe that the PCEPA has forced sex workers to work in unsafe environments.

Crime investigators seem far less interested in tracking down murderers of sex workers than in solving homicides that do not involve a sex worker. According to Statistics Canada, 294 sex workers in Canada were murdered between 1991 and 2014. One in three of those homicides remains unsolved—a noticeably greater proportion than for homicides not involving a sex worker, which is one in five. Prostitution is one of the world's most dangerous professions. In the United States the death rate is 204 for every 100,000 prostitutes—that is nearly ten times the death rate for American women in general.

I AM A FEMINIST

Sex work is a controversial topic. There are those who believe we must eliminate sex work; other people believe we must focus on doing all we can to protect the rights of sex workers. Even in countries such as the Netherlands, where prostitution is legal, sex workers remain marginalized. Children may be forced or sold into prostitution. According to ChildRight, the number of prostituted children in the Netherlands rose from 4,000 in 1996 to 15,000 in 2001. Many of those children were trafficked from other countries. The Dutch government has been taking action to fight the trafficking of children. In 2005 the maximum penalty for human trafficking in the Netherlands was six years. In 2013 that penalty was increased to twelve years. Since 2013 specialized judges have been handling human-trafficking cases in the Netherlands.

Heather Jarvis is program coordinator for the Safe Harbour Outreach Project (SHOP), a sex-worker advocacy program in St. John's, Newfoundland. Since SHOP was established in 2013, it has assisted over 200 clients, most of whom are women. Jarvis told me that she has learned a great deal from her clients. "The women I get to work with are some of the most creative, resourceful, resilient, funny and knowledgeable people I've ever met. They are so much more than sex workers. They are mothers, PhD students, they are Indigenous, they're queer and trans women. They're amazing," she said.

*Chapter Seven*

# RAISING FEMINIST BOYS: ALLIES IN THE FIGHT AGAINST SEXISM

**"I**'m a feminist," Michael told me during an interview at a Montreal café.

Michael, who was eighteen at the time of our talk, works at the tennis club near my house in the summers. His mom is Sue Montgomery, one of the two journalists behind #BeenRapedNeverReported. Not all boys and young men, or older men for that matter, are willing to declare themselves feminists. In the spring of 2017 Michael was invited back to his old high school, along with his mother and older sister, Molly, to address the school's feminist club.

"My mom did most of the talking," Michael said. But after Montgomery's presentation, the session turned into an open discussion about raising feminist sons.

Michael has witnessed sexism at his workplace. One rainy morning Michael and a female co-worker named Louise were maintaining the grass courts. "The courts were soft, so we couldn't let people on. A member complained when Louise told him he couldn't play. So the guy ignored her and went to talk to another male employee who knew less than Louise did," said Michael. The male employee, who had not seen the condition of the courts, told the man he could play tennis. "Louise told him he couldn't. Then the guy began berating her. In the end, the manager of the club—who happens to be a woman—came out and said, *If Louise said the courts aren't ready, you can't go on.*" Only at that point did the man finally relent.

In this chapter we will look at some of the ways boys can be raised so that, like Michael and Canadian prime minister Justin Trudeau and many others, they will become feminists. This includes encouraging them to express emotion, to consider working at jobs that are not traditionally male, to make a habit of doing household chores, to form genuine friendships with members of both sexes and to resist what is sometimes called **rape culture.**

More and more men realize they need to speak up and voice their support for feminism

## HOLLERING BACK AT HARASSMENT: HOLLABACK!

In 2005 New Yorker Emily May co-founded Hollaback!, a global online platform to end harassment. In a telephone interview May told me that most girls experience harassment for the first time at around the age of puberty. "Young people often feel it's their fault. They may feel they can't tell their parents because they are afraid their parents will never let them outside again. Young people need to know the harassment is not their fault. You didn't do anything to cause it. You're not alone."

The ihollaback.org website is a place for individuals who have been harassed to share their experiences. Since the website went live over 10,000 girls and women have posted their stories. Hollaback! also provides training workshops to help deal with and prevent harassment. The project began in New York City and has spread to 50 cities in 25 countries. The Hollaback! manifesto begins by stating, "We all have the right to be who we are wherever we are." It goes on to promise that "this world will have more than just absence of harassment. People will have conversations that bridge difference."

Sharing stories, said May, benefits both the individual and the world. "Telling their stories helps girls and women understand that 'this happened to me, but this is also about the world we live in.'"

I asked May whether she thinks girls and women who are harassed should respond at the time of the incident. May said there are many ways to deal with harassment, including sharing what happened later with a friend or family member, journaling about it or posting it online. "If you choose to have [an immediate] response, that's your choice. It doesn't have to be in the moment. If you do choose to respond in the moment, assess your safety. If you feel comfortable, look the person in the eye and say, 'What you just said isn't okay or appropriate.' Don't engage in a conversation. You're not a one-woman street-harassment education machine."

## EXPRESS EMOTION

I've already told you about psychology professor Michael Climan, who is the father of two sons, now thirty and thirty-three years old. Unlike many other dads (and some moms too), Climan never tried to stop his sons from crying. He never told them, "Crying is for wusses" or "Don't be a sissy" or "Man up."

"Everybody should cry," Climan told me. "Boys need to be able to express what they feel."

For too long boys were taught that it's wrong to cry. But repressing emotions can lead to unhappiness and anger.

And yet, even in the twenty-first century, some boys and men are not comfortable expressing their emotions. Many are reluctant to cry in public.

Thomas, thirteen, said that when he was in elementary school there was pressure from the other boys not to cry. "Some guys made a competition out of who cried the least. They counted how many times they had cried in their lives. One guy said he'd never cried in his life," Thomas recalled.

The day I met him, at his school's feminist club, he was not at all ashamed to admit that he sometimes cries. "I cry when I get stressed out. My parents say it's okay, to let it out," he said.

The topic of how difficult it is for some men and boys to cry has come up in my classroom too. Many of my male students say they were discouraged from crying when they were growing up. Some say they cannot remember the last time they cried.

And some of my female students have admitted they feel uncomfortable when they see a boy or man cry! This is an indication that girls and women must also support boys and men when they express emotion.

Esme, sixteen, who helps run her school's feminist club, said that some of her male friends have told her they wish they could cry, only they don't know how to do it. "It's like we need to teach crying," said Esme.

We don't only cry when we are sad. We cry when we are happy or relieved or angry. When we deny or repress feelings, we may lose touch with who we are. The inability to express emotion can lead to frustration and anger—emotions many boys and men find easier to express.

Former United States president Barack Obama showed us that it is not only okay for men to cry, but that it's also healthy and important. The day before he was elected to the White House in 2008, his grandmother died. Speaking about her to a crowd in North Carolina, Obama teared up. He also cried during his 2012 speech about the murders of twenty children and six adults at Sandy Hook Elementary School in Newtown, Connecticut. Obama cried, too, during a tribute speech to his wife, Michelle. True strength does not come from repressing feelings and maintaining a tough exterior; it comes from expressing our vulnerability. Thanks, Mr. Obama, for showing us how it's done!

## BIG BOYS *DO* CRY

Telling boys to "man up" is the same as telling them to block out their emotions. Repressing feelings can lead to anger and depression—and sometimes even suicide. Though teenage girls are more likely than teenage boys to attempt suicide, boys are four times more likely than girls to die from suicide. So what can we tell boys instead of "man up"?

Dana Kasper, founder of the Child and Family Counseling Center of Columbus in Ohio, believes we all need to express our feelings. "Emotions tell us we are alive," she said in a 2017 interview with the *Huffington Post*. Kasper recommends that parents model the healthy expression of emotions for their children. She also recommends a daily debriefing session in which family members not only discuss what happened during their day, but also share their feelings.

We need more male teachers in elementary schools and early childhood education. These men are important role models, demonstrating that men too can be nurturers.

## NONTRADITIONAL CAREERS FOR MEN

When Martine Bégin, vice-president of Quebec's Pay Equity Commission, was growing up, a guidance counselor told her she could never become a pilot—because she was a girl.

Boys get similar messages about careers that are seen as traditionally female. What's it like to be a male ballet dancer, male nurse or male elementary schoolteacher? These are all professions that have long been associated with women.

We know that children benefit from exposure to diversity. Seeing a male ballet dancer perform, being treated by a male nurse or having a male elementary schoolteacher can help challenge gender stereotypes.

Yet male elementary schoolteachers often report being treated with a certain suspicion, particularly by parents. While it is not uncommon for female elementary schoolteachers to hug their students, most male teachers avoid giving hugs because they do not want to risk being accused of inappropriate conduct. In the world of education, most sexual-abuse allegations are against male teachers. Fear of such accusations is often cited as a reason men are reluctant to teach at the elementary level.

## MALE ROLE MODELS NEEDED
### Nick von Roretz is a feminist!

"I've been called Dad more than once. I've also been called Mom," said Nick von Roretz, 30, who teaches grades three and four. Von Roretz is the only male homeroom teacher at his school (there are two male gym teachers and a male science specialist). "I know I'm a minority in the field," he told me. No one has ever given von Roretz flak for his choice of profession, but he said, "Friends have asked me, 'Have you ever considered high school?'"

Von Roretz was 22 when he began teaching elementary school. "On my first day a little boy had a toilet accident. He asked for help. I didn't feel comfortable so I asked a female co-worker for help," von Roretz recalled. Now, as a more experienced teacher, von Roretz would have no qualms about helping the little boy. "But I would never do that for a little girl," he added. Hugging kids is not an issue for von Roretz. "I'm not a hugger. But if a child comes for a hug, I'll hug back," he said.

In the past basic household chores such as washing dishes and folding laundry were seen as women's work. Thank goodness that's changing!

## SAY YES TO HOUSEHOLD CHORES

Michael knows his way around the kitchen. He can make a mean breakfast. Another one of his specialties is tofu with spicy peanut sauce, bok choy and rice.

At Michael's home, his mom does most of the cooking ("She loves cooking," Michael said), but Michael's dad does plenty of other chores—including cleanup and laundry. "From what I can see, it's pretty even," said Michael.

Studies indicate that when partners divide up chores equitably, their relationship has a better chance of success. One of the most common causes of tension in a relationship is when one partner feels she or he is doing more than her or his fair share of household tasks and child-rearing.

But saying yes to household chores has even wider-reaching benefits. When fathers help around the house and with child-rearing, they provide healthy role models. And, inevitably, fathers who are actively involved in childcare forge closer relationships with their kids.

Of course, not all families are like Michael's. My father only learned his way around the kitchen when he was in his eighties and my mother had become too frail to cook. In some cultures it is still customary for girls and women to prepare food, serve it and collect and wash the dishes after a meal. It is not hard to imagine that a boy in such a family might resist change. After all, who doesn't like being served?

But if we want to create a more equitable world, if we want families to thrive, boys and men need to pitch in too.

So here's a question for boys and men around the world: Are you cooking tonight or doing the cleanup?

## FOSTER GENUINE FRIENDSHIPS

There's a famous Beatles song that includes the line *I get by with a little help from my friends.*

Friends are the family we choose for ourselves.

A friend is someone with whom you can be your true self, with whom you laugh and cry (remember the importance of crying?) and vent. And a real friend will make you a better person, because a real friend will tell you the truth when you need to hear it.

We know that children with good friends have higher self-esteem and are better able to cope with stress. People who are lonely or isolated are more likely to become depressed. They even have shorter life-spans.

Girls are socialized to develop friendships. Have you ever noticed how the acronym BFF (best friend forever) is almost exclusively used by girls?

In our culture, boys are "buds" or "bros." They are more likely to give each other high fives or fist bumps than hugs. In general, boys are less likely than girls to confide in their friends. Perhaps that relates to how boys are socialized not to show vulnerability.

Niobe Way, a professor of applied psychology at New York University and author of *Deep Secrets: Boys' Friendships and the Crisis of Connection*, has observed that as boys grow up, their friendships with other males often fall to the side. "As boys reach manhood, they begin to lose their closest male friends and become less willing to be emotionally expressive because they associate these qualities with being female or gay. They also become more isolated and lonely and, according to national data, five times more likely to commit suicide than girls."

Make a friend. Be a friend.

How else are we supposed to get by?

## RESIST RAPE CULTURE

*Rape culture* refers to the trivialization of male violence against women and to the blaming of victims. Rape culture is so common that all too often it goes unnoticed.

For instance, when someone makes a joke about rape, that spreads and reinforces rape culture. In the fall of 2017, during a high school football game in South Carolina, four male students spelled out the word *RAPE* with spray-painted letters on their chests. A group of concerned parents turned to social media to condemn the boys' behavior. In their post the parents wrote, *The assumption these young men seem to have made is that their*

We need to raise consciousness about rape culture. Speaking up when you hear a rape joke and taking part in protests are ways of raising consciousness and creating change.

*position and privilege allows them to make "jokes" about rape as a viable threat.*

When someone is told a joke about rape and does not object to the joke, that also promotes rape culture. Speaking up for each other is the best way to resist rape culture.

That's what Michael did when he witnessed signs of rape culture at a recent gathering of friends. "One guy was talking to a girl. His twin brother said, *They're gonna hook up.* One of the girl's friends said, *She's not really interested in him.* Then the guy's brother observed, *Oh, she should [hook up with him]*."

Michael decided to speak up. "I was baffled, so I told the guy's brother, *She has no obligation to do anything. They're just talking.*"

Of course it isn't always easy to stand up for what's right. But Michael is aware that as a healthy, young, educated, middle-class, white male, he has many privileges. "I recognize that I have a lot of opportunities. I don't feel guilty about that. But I feel I have an obligation to use these opportunities as a way to help others," he told me.

Speak up, too, when you see ads that objectify women or you hear misogynistic song lyrics. Here are some examples of the latter:

• In 1987 Guns N' Roses came out with a song called "It's So Easy" that included the disturbing lines *Turn around, bitch. I got a use for you/ Besides you ain't got nothing better to do/ And I'm bored.*
• In 1992 Sublime released a song actually entitled "Date Rape."
• In 1994 rapper Bizarre put out a song that included these lyrics: *My little sister's birthday/She'll remember me/For a gift I had ten of my boys take her virginity.*
• In 2013 Rick Ross boasted in rap artist Rocko's track "U.O.E.N.O." about raping someone who's been drugged: *Put Molly all in her champagne, she ain't even know it/I took her home and I enjoyed that, she ain't even know it.*
• And in 2015 Justin Bieber promoted date-rape culture in his song "What Do You Mean?": *What do you mean, when you nod your head yes/But you wanna say no?/When you don't want me to move/But you tell me to go.*

Which brings us back to the subject of consent. Classroom sex education has tended to focus on issues like safe sex and sexually transmitted disease. But we also need to discuss consent, which, when it comes to sex, means agreeing *very clearly* to engage in a sexual activity. Healthy sexual relationships are consensual. No means no. This does not change regardless of what a girl happens to be wearing or whether she has consumed alcohol or drugs.

In *Feminism: Reinventing the F-Word*, Nadia Abushanab Higgins writes that she prefers the expression *Yes means yes* over *No means no.* "Also known as affirmative consent, 'Yes means yes!' says that sexual consent requires more than just the absence of the word *no* to reject a sexual encounter. It requires a clear yes from partners to express willingness to have sex," she writes.

## LOW-CUT TOPS AND SHORT SKIRTS—
## A FASHION STATEMENT, NOT AN INVITATION TO RAPE

"What were you wearing?" It's a question too many rape victims are asked, and it implies that how they were dressed may have indicated they were open to having sex. "What Were You Wearing?" was also the name of a powerful art installation exhibited in September 2017 at the University of Kansas's student union building. The installation featured 18 outfits, displayed next to the stories of 18 rape survivors. The clothing was not the actual clothing worn by the women when they were raped, but was based on their descriptions of what they were wearing. In an interview with the *Chicago Tribune*, Jen Brockman, director of the university's Sexual Assault, Prevention and Education Center, explained the purpose of the exhibit. "We're hoping students can see that this narrative they're fed—that someone's clothing causes sexual violence—is false."

The first SlutWalk took place in Toronto, ON, in 2011. It was a way to protest rape culture and victim blaming. Since then the SlutWalk movement has grown, with SlutWalks taking place around the world.

## LET'S WALK THE TALK!

*Slutwalk* is the name for a protest march calling for the end of rape culture, victim blaming and slut shaming. Slutwalks have taken place around the world in such countries as Brazil and Switzerland. But slutwalks are a Canadian invention. It all started during a talk at York University's Osgoode Hall Law School in 2011, when Toronto police constable Michael Sanguinetti commented, "I've been told I'm not supposed to say this—however, women should avoid dressing like sluts in order not to be victimized."

That comment inspired Heather Jarvis and Sonya JF Barnett to organize a slutwalk in Toronto's Queen's Park in April 2011. The organizers expected about 100 protesters to turn up. Instead 3,000 people participated. Those protesters did not know that they were creating an international movement.

During a telephone interview, Jarvis, who now lives in St. John's, Newfoundland (you met her in chapter 6, where she talked about her work with the Safe Harbour Outreach Project), told me she is often asked why she and Barnett called their event a slutwalk. "We picked up the language of that police officer and threw it back," she said. Jarvis also explained that there is no dress code for a slutwalk. "Dress as you're comfortable. This happens to us no matter what we wear. We want to challenge how the real or perceived way that girls or women dress is used as a justification to treat them badly or even to hurt them," she said.

Jarvis thinks it is both terrible and wonderful that slutwalks have become a global movement. "It's terrible because it's devastating that these problems are so widespread. It's wonderful to see this much grassroots action in response and to see so many people come together," she said.

# A FINAL WORD FROM THE AUTHOR

What I'm about to say sounds dramatic, but it's 100 percent true. Writing this book has been a life-changing experience.

On a personal level it's made me rethink many of my own attitudes, such as my focus on appearance (my own and others), my competitiveness with other women and my old thinking that I need a romantic partner to be happy.

I have always been good at standing up for others, but I have not always been so good at standing up for myself. That is changing too.

Researching and writing this book has stirred up a lot of feelings for me. Many days while I was working on it I felt sad and angry. There is still so much inequality in the world. Too many girls and women remain at risk of mistreatment and even death.

At the same time I realized that, despite whatever challenges I've faced, in many ways I'm spoiled. I have privileges many women lack—such as an education and a job that is satisfying and allows me to support myself.

I also found myself feeling oddly hopeful. In fact the more work I did—especially around the subject of activism—the more hopeful I felt. Girls, boys, women and men around the world are working together to ensure that we all have equal rights.

And while I was working on this book there have been many important developments in the fight for girls' and women's rights—such as the founding of the #MeToo and Time's Up movements. There has been news, much of it positive, almost every day. Keeping up with the latest developments has kept me busy. There will, no doubt, be many more developments after this book goes to press. It's one of the reasons I've included a list of websites for you to visit after you've read this book. Bookmark the websites so that you can stay up to date, and add your own bookmarks as you continue your exploration of feminism.

Mine is not an innocent, naïve hopefulness. It's more like the first shoot of green that pops up in my garden after a long Montreal winter. Things are not perfect—they may never be perfect. But there are signs of growth. Better days are ahead for all of us if we work together.

I plan to keep learning and reading about feminism and to start participating actively in the work that is ahead.

It is not easy to have conversations about many of the subjects raised in this book. But we need to have those difficult conversations. Girls and women need allies in the fight for equal rights and opportunities. Boys and men can be our allies. We need to be our own allies too.

Together, we can make the world a better place.

We are feminists.

# GLOSSARY

*abolitionist*—a person who is in favor of abolishing a policy such as capital punishment or, in the past, slavery

*advertiser*—a company or person seeking to promote a product or service

*allies*—helpers or supporters

*amatonormativity*—the belief that everybody should be part of a couple

*assimilation*—the process in which a minority group or culture comes to resemble a dominant group

*body image*—how a person sees herself when she looks in the mirror

*body image distortion* or *body dysmorphic disorder*—when people can't see themselves accurately but instead perceive their features and body size as distorted

*body positive*—accepting and appreciating your body as it is

*body shaming*—mocking or humiliating a woman based on her body shape or size

*cisgender*—a person whose sense of identity and gender corresponds with their birth sex

*clitoridectomy* (also known as female genital mutilation [FGM])—total or partial removal of the clitoris, the small, sensitive erectile part of the female genitals

*consciousness-raising groups*—groups that met to draw attention to issues affecting society. During the second wave of feminism, women met in each other's homes to discuss work, family, life, education and sex

*consent*—the voluntary agreement to do something, such as engage in sexual activity

*date rape*—a sexual assault committed during a date

*developed world*—countries in which there is a high level of industrial activity and citizens can earn good wages

*feminism*—the advocacy of women's rights based on equality of the sexes

*first-wave feminism*—the women's movement that began in the 19th century and continued into the early 20th century

*fourth-wave feminism*—the women's movement that began around 2012, with hashtag activism playing an important role

*franchise*—the right to vote in political elections

*glass ceiling*—a metaphor used to describe the invisible barrier that prevents women—and members of minority groups—from rising to the highest ranks in the workplace

*hashtag activism*—using social media platforms to demonstrate support for a cause such as feminism

*heteronormativity*— social structures that assume heterosexuality to be the norm

*hookup*— casual sexual encounter without emotional bonds or long-term commitments

*human rights*— things we are entitled to because we are human and that set out how we can expect to be treated

*intersectionality*—how people's experiences of oppression are shaped by their race, class, gender, ethnicity and sexuality

*intimate partner violence* (also called domestic violence)—emotional and/or physical aggression perpetrated by one's intimate partner

*John*—a male client who purchases sexual services

*marginalized*—used in reference to individuals or communities that are socially disadvantaged and often discriminated against

*maternal morbidity*—any health condition attributed to or worsened by pregnancy and childbirth

*maternal mortality*— death of women during pregnancy and childbirth

*misogyny*—hatred for girls or women

*multiperspectival*—including many perspectives

*nongovernmental organization (NGO)*—any nonprofit, voluntary citizens' group that is organized on a local, national or international level

*not-for-profit organization*—an organization that uses profits to support a cause instead of earning profits for its owners

*objectification*—the act of treating a person as an object or thing

*pay inequity*—discrimination, usually based on gender or race, in the wage-setting system

*pimp*—an individual (usually a man) who controls prostitutes and arranges clients for them, taking part of their earnings in return

*rape culture*—an environment in which prevailing social attitudes normalize or trivialize sexual assault and abuse

*second-wave feminism*—a movement that began in the United States in the 1960s and focused on women's sexuality as well as their roles at home and in the workplace

*sex positive*—an open, positive attitude toward sex and sexuality

*sex slavery/sex trafficking*—kidnapping and moving individuals across national or international borders and then forcing them to work as prostitutes

*sexism*—prejudice or stereotyping based on a person's sex, usually directed at girls or women

*sexual coercion*—gaining sexual cooperation in exchange for job-related outcomes

*sexual double standard*—an attitude that permits sexual freedom and promiscuity for men but not for women

*sexual harassment*—behavior of a sexual nature that a person finds offensive or unwelcome. Can include any unwanted sexual attention—verbal or physical—as well as sexual coercion

*size inclusive*—embracing bodies of all sizes

*slut shaming*—calling a woman a slut for behaving in ways that are judged to be sexually provocative

*slutwalk*—a protest march calling for the end of rape culture, victim blaming and slut shaming

*STEM*—acronym for science, technology, engineering and mathematics

*suffrage*—the right to vote in political elections

*suffragists* (or *suffragettes*)—early feminists who fought for women's right to vote

*temperance movement*—movement advocating moderation in alcohol intake or total abstinence

*third-wave feminism*—movement that began in the late 1990s and focused on intersectionality

*trans inclusive*—acknowledging that some people identify as a gender other than the one they were assigned at birth

*vasectomy*—surgical procedure to sterilize a man

# STAYING UP TO DATE: RESOURCES

Remember how Jessica Valenti said feminism's fourth wave is happening online? If you want to learn even more about feminism, check out these websites.

**Camp fYrefly** (leadership programs for LGBTQ youth across Canada): ualberta.ca/camp-fyrefly

**Canada 2067** (program that supports STEM learning for Canadian students in kindergarten through grade twelve): https://canada2067.ca/en/

**DAWN-RAFH** (DisAbled Women's Network, an important resource for Canadian girls and women with disabilities and those who support them): dawncanada.net/

**Desert Flower Foundation** (dedicated to the eradication of female genital mutilation): desertflowerfoundation.org

**The FBomb** (blog for young feminists, founded by Julie Zeilinger when she was only 16 years old): juliezeilinger.com/thefbomb/

**Feministing** (feminist blog founded by Jessica Valenti in 2004 that addresses young feminists): feministing.com

**Half the Sky** (movement inspired by journalists Nicholas Kristof and Sheryl WuDunn to fight the oppression of girls and women around the world): halftheskymovement.org

**Hollaback** (movement to end harassment and ensure that public spaces are safe for all of us): ihollaback.org

**Jezebel** (current-events blog aimed at women): jezebel.com

**The Malala Fund** (makes it possible for girls around the world to have access to education): malala.org

**Marie Stopes** (provides contraception and safe abortion services to millions of women and families across the world): mariestopes.org

**The National Eating Disorder Information Centre** (useful resource for individuals struggling with eating disorders): http://nedic.ca

**The National Inquiry into Missing and Murdered Indigenous Women and Girls** (recognizes the stories of missing and murdered Indigenous women and girls, helps those who are grieving their losses and investigates how officials handle the cases of MMIWG): mmiwg-ffada.ca/en/

**Native Women's Association of Canada** (works to enhance, promote and foster the social, economic, cultural and political well-being of Indigenous women): nwac.ca.

**Plan Canada** (development organization working to improve the lives of children—check out its Because I Am A Girl blog): plancanada.ca

**Planned Parenthood** (nonprofit organization that provides sexual health care in the United States and globally): plannedparenthood.org

**RAINN** (Rape, Abuse & Incest National Network; the largest American anti-sexual assault organization): https://centers.rainn.org/

**Rupi Kaur** (Canadian poet and artist who explores issues such as abuse and what it means to be a woman): https://rupikaur.com

**Sexted** (Montreal-based anonymous text hotline that helps girls and women understand sexual harassment and how to put a stop to it): https://sexted.org

**She's the First** (fights gender inequality through education): shesthefirst.org

**Strong Women, Strong Girls** (empowers girls to imagine a broader future through a curriculum grounded on female role models): swsg.org

**Time's Up** (movement against sexual harassment, founded on January 1, 2018): timesupnow.com

**Unicef** (School-in-a-Box program): unicef.org/supply/index_40377.html

**WAVAW** (rape crisis center that provides support to end all forms of violence against girls and women, including rape): wavaw.ca. Twenty-four-hours-a-day, toll-free crisis hotline: 1-877-392-7583

**Yes Means Yes** (Project Respect campaign that aims to educate young people about the need for enthusiastic consent): yesmeansyes.com

# REFERENCES

## INTRODUCTION

Baumgardner, Jennifer, and Amy Richards. *FeministA: Young Women, Feminism, and the Future*. 10th Anniversary Edition. New York: Farrar, Straus and Giroux, 2010.

## CHAPTER ONE

Baumgardner, Jennifer, and Amy Richards. *What is Feminism?* New York: Soapbox Inc., 2013.

McNamara, Brittney. "Meet *The New York Times*'s First Gender Editor." *Teen Vogue*, Oct. 10, 2017. teenvogue.com/story/new-york-times-first-gender-editor.

## CHAPTER TWO

Human Rights Watch. "They Burned it All: Destruction of Villages, Killings, and Sexual Violence in Unity State South Sudan." Human Rights Watch, July 22, 2015. hrw.org/report/2015/07/22/they-burned-it-all/destruction-villages-killings-and-sexual-violence-unity-state.

Kristof, Nicholas D., and Sheryl WuDunn. *Half the Sky: Turning Oppression into Opportunity for Women Worldwide*. New York: Vintage Books. 2010.

Plan International. "Sixteen-Year-Old Nyawut Misses at Least One Day of School Every Month because of Her Period." plan.ie/stories/dignity-kits-help-keep-girls-at-school/.

Yousafzai, Malala, with Christina Lamb. *I Am Malala: The Girl Who Stood Up for Education and Was Shot by the Taliban*. London: Orion Publishing, 2013.

## CHAPTER THREE

Black, Frances, Gabriella Kountourides and Laura Ferris. "Apologise For, and Amend the Irresponsible Marketing of Your New Bra Range 'Body.'" Petition at change.org, Oct. 30, 2014. change.org/p/victoriassecret-apologise-for-your-damaging-perfect-body-campaign-iamperfect.

Engeln, Renee. *Beauty Sick: How the Cultural Obsession with Appearance Hurts Girls and Women.* New York: HarperCollins, 2017.

Friday, Nancy. *The Power of Beauty.* New York: HarperCollins, 1996.

Gerstein, Julie. "Here's What the Average Woman in the US Spends on Makeup—and It's a Lot." *BuzzFeed*, March 29, 2017. buzzfeed.com/juliegerstein/heres-what-the-average-american-woman-spends-on-makeup-and?utm_term=.hikkZqGKK#.halO6a9MM.

Petter, Olivia. "John Lewis Gender Neutral Clothing Labels Faces Public Backlash." *The Independent*, Sept. 4, 2017. independent.co.uk/life-style/fashion/john-lewis-gender-neutral-clothing-labels-response-sex-boys-girls-men-women-a7928006.html.

## CHAPTER FOUR

Allen, Sarah, and Kerry Daly. "The Effects of Father Involvement: An Updated Research Summary of the Evidence." University of Guelph, May 2007. fira.ca/cms/documents/29/Effects_of_Father_Involvement.pdf.

Baer, Drake. "There's a Word for the Assumption That Everybody Should Be in a Relationship." *The Cut*, March 8, 2017. thecut.com/2017/03/amatonormativity-everybody-should-be-coupled-up.html.

Bernstein, Elizabeth. "In Two-Career Marriages, Women Still Do More of the Work at Home." *Wall Street Journal*, Sept. 30, 2015. wsj.com/articles/in-two-career-marriages-women-still-do-more-of-the-work-at-home-1443600654.

Burke, David. "Complaints about N.S. Judge Who Said 'A Drunk can Consent' Will Be Investigated." CBC News, Sept. 7, 2017. cbc.ca/news/canada/nova-scotia/judge-gregory-lenehan-drunk-sexual-assault-al-rawi-consent-1.4278905.

Canadian Centre for Justice Statistics. "Family Violence in Canada: A Statistical Profile, 2014." Statistics Canada, Jan. 21, 2016. statcan.gc.ca/pub/85-002-x/2016001/article/14303-eng.pdf.

Cooney, Samantha. "The Azis Ansari Allegation has People Talking about 'Affirmative Consent.' What's That?" *Time*, Jan. 17, 2018. http://time.com/5104010/aziz-ansari-affirmative-consent.

Culp-Ressler, Tara. "Why Rape Prevention Activists Don't Like the New Nail Polish That Can Detect Roofies." *ThinkProgress*, August 25, 2014. https://thinkprogress.org/why-rape-prevention-activists-dont-likethe-new-nail-polish-that-can-detect-roofies-21a1193c14f6/.

Garcia, Justin R. "Sexual Hook-Up Culture." American Psychological Association, February 2013. apa.org/monitor/2013/02/ce-corner.aspx.

Garcia-Moreno, Claudia, Alessandra Guedes and Wendy Knerr. "Understanding and Addressing Violence against Women." World Health Organization, 2012. http://apps.who.int/iris/bitstream/10665/77432/1/WHO_RHR_12.36_eng.pdf.

Geller, Brooke. "Singled Out: Society's Obsession with Love (And Why It's Okay to Be Single)." *Healthyway*, Oct. 19, 2017. healthyway.com/content/singled-out-societys-obsession-with-love-and-why-its-okay-to-be-single.

Ouellet-Morin, Isabelle, et al. "Intimate Partner Violence and New-Onset Depression: A Longitudinal Study of Women's Childhood and Adult Histories of Abuse." *Depression and Anxiety*, March 2015.

Rosenberg, Jeffrey, and W. Bradford Wilcox. "The Importance of Fathers in the Healthy Development of Children." U.S. Department of Health and Human Services, 2006. childwelfare.gov/pubPDFs/fatherhood.pdf.

SexAssault.ca. "Sexual Assault Statistics in Canada." n.d. sexassault.ca/statistics.htm.

Tanenbaum, Leora. *I Am Not a Slut: Slut-Shaming in the Age of the Internet.* New York: Harper Perennial, 2015.

Tanenbaum, Leora. "The Truth about Slut-Shaming." *HuffPost*, April 15, 2015. huffingtonpost.com/leora-tanenbaum/the-truth-about-slut-shaming_b_7054162.html.

Valenti, Jessica. *Full Frontal Feminism: A Young Woman's Guide to Why Feminism Matters.* Berkeley: Seal Press, 2007.

Walters, M.L., et al. "The National Intimate Partner and Sexual Violence Survey." United States Centers for Disease Control and Prevention, Sept. 25, 2017. cdc.gov/violenceprevention/pdf/nisvs_sofindings.pdf.

## CHAPTER FIVE

Abushanab Higgins, Nadia. *Feminism: Reinventing the F-Word.* Minneapolis: Twenty-First Century Books, 2016.

Angus Reid Institute. "Three-in-Ten Canadians Say They've Been Sexually Harassed at Work, But Very Few Have Reported This to Their Employers." Dec. 5, 2014. http://angusreid.org/sexual-harassment/.

Bridge, Mark. "Teach Girls to Code Aged 2, Says Computer Pioneer Dame Stephanie Shirley." *Times UK*, Aug. 21, 2017. thetimes.co.uk/article/bring-girls-into-computing-by-teaching-coding-from-the-age-of-two-2fcz605zx.

CBC News. "Military Sexual Misconduct Due to 'Biological Wiring,' Gen. Tom Lawson Tells CBC News." June 16, 2015. cbc.ca/news/politics/military-sexual-misconduct-due-to-biological-wiring-gen-tom-lawson-tells-cbc-news-1.3115993.

Chan, Melissa. "'Now the Work Really Begins.' Alyssa Milano and Tarana Burke on What's Next for the #MeToo Movement." *Time*, Dec. 6, 2017. http://time.com/5051822/time-person-year-alyssa-milano-tarana-burke/.

Chui, Delphine. "Natalie Portman Was Paid Three Times Less Than This Hollywood Actor." *Marie Claire UK*, Jan. 11, 2017. marieclaire.co.uk/entertainment/natalie-portman-admits-to-this-male-actor-being-paid-more-than-her-465954.

Concordia University News. "Breaking through the Glass Ceiling: Women Make Better Leaders." May 27, 2013. concordia.ca/cunews/main/stories/2013/05/27/breaking-through-the-glass-ceiling.html.

Donlon, Denise. *Fearless As Possible (Under the Circumstances)*. Toronto: Anansi, 2016.

Friend, David. "Safe and Sound: Music Festivals Feel Push to Protect Women in Wake of Recent Assaults." *Montreal Gazette*, Aug.1, 2017, C1.

Gillette, Sam. "Closing the Gender Gap in Technology: How the Founder of Girls Who Code Is Teaching Girls Coding and Confidence." *People*, Aug. 22, 2017. http://people.com/books/girls-who-code-founder-gender-gap-technology/.

Gonsalves, Lisabelle. "14-Year-Old Sindhuga Rajamaran Is the Youngest CEO!" iDiva, March 21, 2011. idiva.com/news-work-life/14yearold-sindhuja-rajamaran-is-the-youngest-ceo/3874.

Hegewisch, Ariane, and Asha DuMonthier. "The Gender Wage Gap: 2015." Institute for Women's Policy Research, Sept. 2016. https://iwpr.org/wp-content/uploads/wpallimport/files/iwpr-export/publications/C446.pdf.

Hemmadi, Murad. "What Canadians Say about Workplace Sexual Harassment: A Major National Study Finds Some Common Ground—and Some Big Gaps." *Canadian Business*, Dec. 4, 2014. canadianbusiness.com/blogs-and-comment/sexual-harassment-in-canada-statistics/.

Houlihan, Rachel, and Seglins, Dave. "RCMP Harassment Claims Could Hit 4,000 in Wake of #MeToo, Lawyers Say." CBC News, Jan. 31, 2018. cbc.ca/news/investigates/rcmp-harassment-claims-could-hit-4-000-in-wake-of-metoo-lawyers-say-1.4510891.

Kadane, Lisa. "The Importance of Male Teachers." *Today's Parent*, Sept. 19, 2017. todaysparent.com/kids/the-importance-of-male-teachers/.

Leah, Rachel. "Here's What Oprah Did When She Found Out Her Women Employees Weren't Getting Paid Fairly." *Salon*, Sept. 7, 2017. salon.com/2017/09/07/heres-what-oprah-did-when-she-found-out-her-women-employees-werent-getting-paid-fairly/?fb_comment_id=1700046416694745_1700552429977477.

Noveck, Jocelyn. "The Year of #MeToo." *Montreal Gazette*, Dec. 28, 2017, C5.

Rich, Motoko. "Why Don't More Men Go into Teaching?" *New York Times*, Sept. 6, 2014. nytimes.com/2014/09/07/sunday-review/why-dont-more-men-go-into-teaching.html.

Russian, Ale. "Amy Schumer Asked Netflix for More Money After Learning What Chris Rock and Dave Chappelle Were Paid." *People*, Aug. 22, 2017. http://people.com/movies/amy-schumer-asked-netflix-for-more-money/.

Scheurer, Jason. "The 77-Cent Gender Wage Gap Lie." *Breitbart News*, March 17, 2014. breitbart.com/big-government/2014/03/17/77-cents-worth-of-lies/.

Setoodeh, Ramin. "Sandra Bullock on Hollywood Sexism, Pay Disparity and 'the Worst Experience' of Her Career." *Variety*, Nov. 10, 2015. http://variety.com/2015/film/news/sandra-bullock-sexism-pay-gap-1201637694/.

Slaughter, Anne-Marie. *Unfinished Business: Women, Men, Work, Family.* Toronto: Random House, 2015.

Speicher, Ashley. "Why Don't More Girls Code?" YouTube video, 1:01. Posted by Microsoft Learning, Nov. 18, 2014. youtube.com/watch?v=iGwC4zfKlS8.

Vagianos, Alanna. "1 in 3 Women Has Been Sexually Harassed at Work, According to Survey." *HuffPost*, Feb.19, 2015. huffingtonpost.ca/entry/1-in-3-women-sexually-harassed-work-cosmopolitan_n_6713814.

Williams, Christine L. *Still a Man's World.* Berkeley: University of California Press, 1995.

## CHAPTER SIX

Blaze Baum, Kathryn, and Matthew McClearn. "Prime Target: How Serial Killers Prey on Indigenous Women." *Globe and Mail*, Nov. 22, 2015. theglobeandmail.com/news/national/prime-targets-serial-killers-and-indigenous-women/article27435090/.

Blue Metropolitan Foundation. *Quebec Roots: Strengthening Communities, The Place I Want to Be 2014–2015.* Montreal: Les éditons Metropolis Bleu, 2015.

CBC News. "LGBT discrimination class actions against federal government merge." March 30, 2017. cbc.ca/news/politics/lgbtq-canada-class-action-1.4047232.

Crenshaw, Kimberlé. "Demarginalizing the Intersection of Race and Sex: A Black Feminist Critique of Antidiscrimination Doctrine, Feminist Theory and Antiracist Politics." *University of Chicago Legal Forum* 1989, no. 1, article 8. https://chicagounbound.uchicago.edu/uclf/vol1989/iss1/8.

d'Entremont, Deidre. "Seeking Justice for Canada's 500 Missing Native Women." *Cultural Survival Quarterly Magazine*, September 2004. culturalsurvival.org/publications/cultural-survival-quarterly/seeking-justice-canadas-500-missing-native-women.

DisAbled Women's Network. "Women with Disabilities and Poverty." DAWN-RAFH Canada fact sheet, n.d. dawncanada.net/ppbdp-en/fact%20sheets/.

Dockterman, Eliana. "Read the Full Transcript of *Master of None* Writer Lena Waithe's Moving Emmys Speech." *Time*, Sept.18, 2017. time.com/4945661/lena-waithe-emmys-speech-master-of-none/.

Hamm, Nia. "Against All Odds: Economic Inequities for Black Women Cripple Communities." NBC News, July 7, 2015. nbcnews.com/news/nbcblk/against-all-odds-economic-inequities-black-women-cripple-communities-n388366.

Harris, Kathleen. "'Our Collective Shame': Trudeau Delivers Historic Apology to LGBT Canadians." CBC News, Nov. 28, 2017. cbc.ca/news/politics/homosexual-offences-expunge-records-1.4422546.

Hill Collins, Patricia. *Black Feminist Thought: Knowledge, Consciousness and the Politics of Empowerment*. New York: Routledge, 1990.

hooks, bell. *Feminism is for Everybody: Passionate Politics*. Cambridge, MA: South End Press, 2000.

Indian Law Resource Center. "Ending Violence against Native Women." N.d. http://indianlaw.org/issue/ending-violence-against-native-women.

Kielburger, Craig and Marc. "Path to Reconciliation: One Toronto School Is Helping Foster Understanding." *Montreal Gazette*, July 4, 2017, C2.

Native Women's Association of Canada. "Fact Sheet: Missing and Murdered Aboriginal Women and Girls." 2010. nwac.ca/wp-content/uploads/2015/05/Fact_Sheet_Missing_and_Murdered_Aboriginal_Women_and_Girls.pdf.

Neal, Brandi. "Wage Gap Statistics You Need to Know on Black Women's Equal Pay Day." *Bustle*, July 30, 2017. bustle.com/p/wage-gap-statistics-you-need-to-know-on-black-womens-equal-pay-day-73403.

Postmedia News. "Most Sex Workers Satisfied with Their Jobs and Don't See Themselves as Victims, Survey Finds." *National Post*, Sept. 23, 2014. http://nationalpost.com/news/canada/most-sex-workers-satisfied-with-their-jobs-and-dont-see-themselves-as-victims-survey-finds.

Rotenberg, Cristine. "Prostitution Offences in Canada: Statistical Trends." Statistics Canada, Nov. 10, 2016. statcan.gc.ca/pub/85-002-x/2016001/article/14670-eng.htm.

Sears, Brad, and Lee Badgett. "Beyond Stereotypes: Poverty in the LGBT Community." *Tides-Momentum* 4 (June 2012), The Williams Institute, UCLA School of Law. https://williamsinstitute.law.ucla.edu/headlines/beyond-stereotypes-poverty-in-the-lgbt-community/.

Tiggeloven, Carin. "Child Prostitution in the Netherlands." Radio Netherlands, Dec. 18, 2001. prostitutionresearch.com/Child%20prostitution%20in%20the%20Netherlands.pdf.

Truth and Reconciliation Commission of Canada. *Truth and Reconciliation Commission of Canada: Calls to Action.* Truth and Reconciliation Commission of Canada report, 2015. trc.ca/websites/trcinstitution/File/2015/Findings/Calls_to_Action_English2.pdf.


## CHAPTER SEVEN

Abushanab Higgins, Nadia. *Feminism: Reinventing the F-Word.* Minneapolis: Twenty-First Century Books, 2016.

Coles, Terri. "10 Tips on Helping Teen Boys Express Their Feelings." *HuffPost*, Feb. 28, 2017. huffingtonpost.ca/2017/02/28/teen-boys-express-feelings_n_15065192.html.

Kadane, Lisa. "The Importance of Male Teachers." *Today's Parent*, Sept. 19, 2017. todaysparent.com/kids/the-importance-of-male-teachers/.

Vagianos, Alanna. "Art Exhibit Powerfully Answers the Question 'What Were You Wearing?'" *HuffPost*, Sept. 14, 2017. huffingtonpost.ca/entry/powerful-art-exhibit-powerfully-answers-the-question-what-were-you-wearing_us_59baddd2e4b02da0e1405d2a.

Vagianos, Alanna. "High School Boys Make 'Rape' Joke at Breast Cancer Awareness Football Game." *HuffPost*, Sept. 20, 2017. huffingtonpost.ca/entry/high-school-boys-make-rape-joke-at-breast-cancer-awareness-football-game_us_59c269fae4b0f22c4a8dfc51.

Way, Niobe. *Deep Secrets: Boys' Friendships and the Crisis of Connection.* Cambridge, MA: Harvard University Press, 2011.

# PHOTO CREDITS

# ACKNOWLEDGMENTS

A giant thank-you to the many people who agreed to be interviewed for this book. I learned so much from all of you. Thanks, as always, to my editor, Sarah Harvey, who asked me to tackle this subject and challenged me to learn more and ask tougher questions. Special thanks to my former student, now a teacher, Maria Di Scala, for reviewing the manuscript so carefully. Thanks to Kennedy Cullen for her valuable input. Huge thanks to Orca art director Teresa Bubela for believing so much in this book and for making it so beautiful. And thanks to illustrator Meags Fitzgerald for the captivating interior illustrations. Thanks, too, to my daughter, Alicia Melamed, for being my anchor—and my role model.

# INDEX

Malala Day, **40**
male attitudes
  allies, 17, 133, 141–151
  emotional expression,
    144–145
  empathy exercise, 118
  and marriage, 88–89,
    148
  objectification of women,
    57
  and pay equity, 97–98
  and sexism, 20, 105,
    150–152
  toward harassment, 111
  toward menstruation,
    60, 75
  toward prostitutes,
    48–49
Mardini, Yusra, 47
marginalized communities,
  15, 29, 48–49. *See also*
  intersectionality
Marie Stopes International
  (MSI), **42**, 43, 162
marketing, 54, 55, 58–59
marriage, 73, 88–89, 132. *See
  also* family
May, Emily, 143
McClung, Nellie, 19
media. *See also* social media
  and activism, 26, 31, 67,
    **79**, 112
  and advertising, 54, 55,
    58–59
  new reporters, 30, 97, 115
menstruation, 38, 60, 63,
  65, 75
mentors, female, 106, 108
Messing, Debra, 96
Milano, Alyssa, 112
misogyny, 9, 109, 154
Missing and Murdered
  Indigenous Women and
  Girls (MMIWG), 124–125,
  128, 162
Molly-Beth (youth
  interview), **62**, 63–64
Montgomery, Michael
  (youth interview), 141–142,
  148–149, 151
Montgomery, Sue, 80, 141
Morgan, Joanne, **10**, 11
Mozambique, impact of
  war, 46
*Ms. Magazine*, 26
music industry, 107, 109, 152

nail polish, to detect date-
  rape drugs, 82

Nakuset, 122, **123**, 127
Native Americans. *See*
  Indigenous community
Native Women's Association
  of Canada (NWAC), 124,
  126, 128, 162
Netherlands, prostitution
  laws, 139
Nobody Left Outside
  (UNHCR), 47
nursing profession, 100, 146

Obama, Barack, 145

parenting, 52, 88–89
Parsons, Rehtaeh, 78
pay inequity, 9, 94–98
Polak, Monique, personal
  experiences, 13, 15, 52–54,
  81, 83–84, 92–93
Portman, Natalie, 96
poverty
  and discrimination, 121,
    122, 129
  and education, 38
  and low-paying jobs,
    91, 109
pregnancy and childbirth.
  *See* reproductive rights
professional jobs, 24, 99–
  105, 108
Project Respect, 76, **77**, 162
Project Unbreakable, **79**
prostitution
  sex slavery, 46, 48–49, 139
  sex trade workers,
    137–139
puberty, 62–63, 143

racism, 22–23, 29, 120–128
Rajamaran, Sindhuja, 108
rape, 72, 74–76, 78–83, 152
rape culture, 150–152
reconciliation, 123
Reddy, Anita, 118
REDress Project, **125**
Redstockings, **24**
refugees, **39**, **46**, 47
relationships
  abusive, 73, 84–87
  cycle of violence, 85–87
  friendship, 149–150
  marriage roles, 88–89,
    148–149
  romantic, 69–72
  sexual consent, 72,
    74–76, 152
reproductive rights, 24, 26,
  41–43

residential schools, 122–124,
  126
resources
  crisis hotline, 76, 87
  glossary, 158–160
  social media, 31, 54,
    67, 79
  websites, 67, 81, 161–162
Richards, Amy, 8, 89
robots, Lego, 104–105
Royal Canadian Mounted
  Police (RCMP), 110–111
Rwanda, impact of war, 46

Sadler, Catt, 97
Safe Harbour Outreach
  Project, 139
Safe Women, Strong Nations
  project, 126
Samantha (youth interview),
  7, 10–11
Scheurer, Jason, 97–98
School-in-a Box (UNICEF),
  162
schools. *See* education
Schumer, Amy, 96
self-esteem
  and body image, 57,
    62–65, 66–67, 109
  impact of advertising, 54,
    58–59
  of males, 63
  and social media, 60–61,
    78
  and suicide, 80, 129,
    145, 150
sex education, 43, 152
sexism, examples of, 9–11,
  141–142
sex positive, 31
sex slavery (trafficking), 46,
  48–49, 139
sex trade workers, 137–139
sexual assault. *See also*
  violence against women
  and choice of clothing,
    **153**, 154–155
  and the courts, 75
  crisis hotline, 76, 87, 162
  date rape, 78–83
  harassment, 22, 110–115,
    143
  and lack of consent, 72,
    74–76, 115, 152
  statistics on, 81
sexual harassment, 22,
  110–115, 143
sexuality, 69–78, 152
She's the First, 37, 162

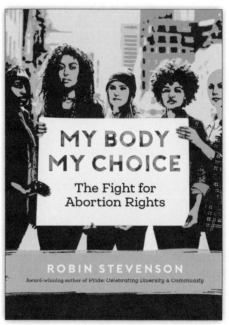

9781459817128 • $19.95 PAPERBACK WITH FLAPS

Abortion is one of the most common of all medical procedures. But it is still stigmatized, and too often people do not feel they can talk about their experiences. Making abortion illegal or hard to access doesn't make it any less common; it just makes it dangerous. People who support abortion rights have been fighting hard to create a world in which the right to access safe and legal abortion services is guaranteed. The opposition to this has been intense and sometimes violent, and victories have been hard-won. The long fight for abortion rights is being picked up by a **new generation of courageous, creative and passionate activists**. This book is about the history, and the future, of that fight.